BHAGAVAD GITA CYCLE OF BIRTH AND DEATH

ARVIND UPADHYAY

Contents

Contents

Preface

The modern man in this present decade of the second half of the 20th century is greatly in need of an effective guide to light. He is groping. He sees only problems everywhere and no solutions are to be found anywhere. He does not know which way to turn, what course to adopt and how to move towards a better state of things. Therefore, his life is filled with restlessness, unhappiness and complication. The Bhagavad Gita contains words of wisdom and practical teachings that contain the answers to the above-mentioned condition of the present-day individual. The Bhagavad Gita is a message addressed to each and every human individual to help him or her to solve the vexing problem of overcoming the present and progressing towards a bright future. This holy scripture is not just an "old scripture", nor is it just a book of "religious teachings", nor even a Hindu holy book. It transcends the bounds of any particular religion or race, and is actually divine wisdom addressed to mankind for all times, in order to help human beings face and solve the ever-present problems of birth and death, of pain, suffering, fear, bondage, love and hate. It enables man to liberate himself from all limiting factors and reach a state of perfect balance, inner stability and mental peace, complete freedom from grief, fear and anxiety. Within its eighteen chapters is revealed a human drama. This is the experience of everyone in this world, the drama of the ascent of man from a state of utter dejection, sorrow and total breakdown and hopelessness to a state of perfect understanding, clarity, renewed strength and triumph. Each discourse holds for you an invaluable new lesson and imparts a new understanding of yourself in a marvellous way. The mystery of man, this world and God, is explained as perhaps nowhere else. The workings of your mind—the real problem to your welfare and happiness—how to overcome it, what the path to blessedness is, as also the path to perdition, the secret of self-mastery and the way to peace amidst your daily activities and duties—all these and more you will find in this great treasure. It is yours by which to enrich your life. To the Western reader I would suggest that he carefully reads through the entire book once. Then he should commence it a second time. Upon the second reading he should adopt the method of selectivity, not in reading but in what he takes from it. Such things as seem to be particularly Hindu and therefore, perhaps, not acceptable to him as a person of another faith, he can just pass by without being perturbed.

But everything else that is of a purely philosophical, psychological, ethical and psychical nature,—all these he can grasp and assimilate fully. He will be wonderfully enriched and supremely blessed. His life will become new from that moment. All clouds will vanish. Light will fill the heart and mind. I assure him of this. This is the Gita. I commend this wonderful gift of God unto every man and woman, towards his or her supreme blessedness and highest welfare. The Srimad Bhagavad Gita is a dialogue between Lord Krishna and Arjuna, narrated in the Bhishma Parva of the Mahabharata. It comprises eighteen discourses of a total of 701 Sanskrit verses. A considerable volume of material has been compressed within these verses. On the battlefield of Kurukshetra, Sri Krishna, during the course of His most instructive and interesting talk with Arjuna, revealed profound, sublime and soul-stirring spiritual truths, and expounded the rare secrets of Yoga, Vedanta, Bhakti and Karma. All the teachings of Lord Krishna were subsequently recorded as the Song Celestial or Srimad Bhagavad Gita by Bhagavan Vyasa for the benefit of humanity at large. The world is under a great debt of gratitude to Bhagavan Vyasa who presented this Song Celestial to humanity for the guidance of their daily conduct of life, spiritual upliftment and Self-realisation. Those who are self-controlled and who are endowed with faith can reap the full benefit of the Gita, which is the science of the Soul. The Gita Jayanti (birthdate of the Gita) is celebrated throughout India by the admirers and lovers of this unique book on the 11th day (Ekadashi) of the bright half of the month of Margasirsha according to the Hindu almanac. It was the day on which the scripture was revealed to the world by Sanjaya. In all the spiritual literature of the world there is no book so elevating and inspiring as the Gita. It expounds very lucidly the cardinal principles or the fundamentals of the Hindu religion and Hindu Dharma. It is the source of all wisdom. It is your great guide. It is your supreme teacher. It is an inexhaustible spiritual treasure. It is a fountain of bliss. It is an ocean of knowledge. It is full of divine splendour and grandeur. The Gita is the cream of the Vedas. It is the essence of the soul-elevating Upanishads. It is a universal scripture applicable to people of all temperaments and for all times. It is a wonderful book with sublime thoughts and practical instructions on Yoga, devotion, Vedanta and action. It is a marvellous book, profound in thought and sublime in heights of vision. It brings peace and solace to souls that are afflicted by the three fires of mortal existence, namely, afflictions caused by one's own body, those caused by beings around one, and those caused by the gods. The Gita contains the divine nectar. It is the wish-fulfilling gem, tree and cow. You can milk anything from it. It is a book for eternity. It is not a catch-penny book, with life like that of a mushroom. It can be one's constant companion of life. It is a vade-mecum for all. Peace, bliss, wisdom, Brahman, Nirvana, Param Padam and Gita are all synonymous terms. The Gita is a boundless ocean of nectar. It is the immortal celestial fruit of the Upanishadic tree. In this unique book you will find an unbiased exposition of the philosophy of action, devotion and knowledge, together with a wonderfully woven synthesis of these three. The Gita is a rare and splendid flower that wafts its sweet aroma throughout the world. If all the Upanishads should represent cows, Sri Krishna is their milker. Arjuna is the calf who first tasted that milk of wisdom of the Self, milked by the divine Cowherd for the benefit of all humanity. This milk is the Bhagavad Gita. It solves not only Arjuna's problems and doubts, but also the world's problems and those of every individual. Glory to Krishna, the friend of the cowherds of Gokula, the joy of Devaki! He who drinks the nectar of the Gita through purification of the heart and regular meditation, attains immortality, eternal bliss, everlasting peace and perennial joy. There is nothing more to be attained beyond this. Just as the dark unfathomed depths of the ocean contain most precious pearls, so also the Bhagavad Gita contains spiritual gems of incalculable value. You will have to dive deep into its depths with a sincere attitude of reverence and faith. Only then will you be able to collect its spiritual pearls and comprehend its infinitely profound and subtle teachings. The Bhagavad Gita is a unique book for all ages. It is one of the most authoritative books of the Hindu religion. It is the immortal song of the Soul, which bespeaks of the glory of life. The instructions given by Sri Krishna are for the whole world. It is a standard book on Yoga for all mankind. The language is as simple as could be. Even a man who has an elementary knowledge of Sanskrit can go through the book. There are numerous commentaries on the Gita at the present time. A volume can be written on each verse. A busy man with an active temperament will be greatly benefited by the commentary of Sri Gangadhar Lokamanya Tilak, entitled Gita Rahasya. A man of devotional temperament will be attracted by Sri Sridhara's commentary, and a man of reason by that of Sri Shankara. The Gita is like an ocean. Sri Shankara, Sri Ramanuja and Sri Madhava dived into it and gave accounts of their interpretation and established their own philosophy. Anyone can do the same and bring out the most precious pearls of divine knowledge and give their own interpretation. Glory to the Gita! Glory to the Lord of the Gita!

The teachings of the Gita are broad, universal and sublime. They do not belong to any cult, sect, creed, age or country. They are meant for the people of the whole world. Based on the soul-elevating Upanishads—the ancient wisdom of seers and saints—the Gita prescribes methods which are within the reach of all. It has a message of solace, freedom, salvation, perfection and peace for all human beings. This sacred scripture is like the great Manasarovar lake for monks, renunciates and thirsting aspirants to sport in. It is the ocean of bliss in which seekers of Truth swim with joy and ecstasy. If the philosopher's stone touches a piece of iron even at one point, the whole of it is transformed into gold. Even so, if you live in the spirit of even one verse of the Gita, you will doubtless be transmuted into divinity. All your miseries will come to an end and you will attain the highest goal of life—immortality and eternal peace. The study of the Gita alone is sufficient for daily Swadhyaya (scriptural study). You will find here a solution for all your doubts. The more you study it with devotion and faith, the more you will acquire deeper knowledge, penetrative insight and clear, right thinking. viii The Bhagavad Gita is a gospel for the whole world. It is meant for the generality of mankind. It was given over five thousand years ago by Lord Krishna to Arjuna. None but the Lord Himself can bring out such a marvellous and unprecedented book which gives peace to its readers, which helps and guides them in the attainment of supreme bliss, and which has survived up to the present time. This itself proves clearly that God exists, that He is an embodiment of knowledge, and that one can attain perfection or liberation only by realising God. The world is one huge battlefield. The real Kurukshetra is within you. The battle of the Mahabharata is still raging within. Ignorance is Dhritarashtra; the individual soul is Arjuna; the indweller of your heart is Lord Krishna, the charioteer; the body is the chariot; the senses are the five horses; mind, egoism, mental impressions, senses, cravings, likes and dislikes, lust, jealousy, greed, pride and hypocrisy are your dire enemies. Guide For Study As the Gita contains subtle and profound teachings, you should study it under a qualified teacher, one who is established in the Absolute. Only when studied with great and intense faith, single-minded devotion and purity, will the truths contained therein be revealed unto you like a fruit on the palm of your hand. Good commentaries written by realised sages will also be of immense help to you. Worldly-minded individuals, however intellectual they may be, cannot grasp the essential teachings of the Gita. They enter into unnecessary discussions and useless debates. They cavil and carp at the teachings. Such ignorant people say: "There is no intimate connection between the verses. They are thrown in a disorderly manner. There is a great deal of repetition." If they study the book with reverence and faith under a qualified teacher all their doubts would vanish. They will realise that there is a close connection between the verses in all the chapters. Repetitions in the Gita and the Upanishads are useful repetitions. They are best calculated to create a deep and indelible impression in the mind of the aspirant. Lord Krishna speaks from different levels of consciousness. In the Gita the word "Avyaktam" sometimes refers to primordial Nature and sometimes to the Absolute Para Brahman also. Therefore, the help of a teacher is necessary if you wish to know the right significance of the verses. In the Kathopanishad the term "brick" is used to denote the gods. In the Hatha Yogic texts it is stated: "At the junction of the rivers Yamuna and Ganga there is a young virgin". The esoteric meaning of this is that there is the Sushumna Nadi between the Ida and the Pingala. So, without the help of a Guru, you will not be able to understand the proper meaning of the verses of the Gita. You will be like the man who brought a horse to one who asked for saindava while taking food. The word saindava means salt as well as horse!

CHAPTER ONE

Harmony in the Gita

Man is a composite of three fundamental factors, namely, will, feeling and cognition. There are three kinds of temperament—the active, the emotional and the rational. Even so, there are three Yogas—Jnana Yoga for a person of enquiry and rational temperament, Bhakti Yoga for the emotional temperament, and Karma Yoga for a person of action. One Yoga is as efficacious as the other. The Bhagavad Gita formulates the theories of the three paths without creating any conflict among them. It harmonises most wonderfully the philosophy of action, devotion and knowledge. All three must be harmoniously blended if you wish to attain perfection. You should have the head of Sri Shankara, the heart of Lord Buddha and the hand of King Janaka. The three horses of this body-chariot—action, emotion and intellect—should work in perfect harmony. Only then will it move smoothly and reach the destination safely and quickly. Only then can you rejoice in the Self, sing the song of Soham, be in tune with the Infinite, hear the soundless voice of the Soul and enjoy the sweet music of the eternal Self. The central teaching of the Gita is the attainment of the final beatitude of life—perfection or eternal freedom. This may be achieved by doing one's prescribed duties of life. Lord Krishna says to Arjuna: "Therefore, without attachment, constantly perform action which is duty, for, by performing action without attachment, man verily reaches the Supreme". The Gita is divided into three sections, illustrative of the three terms of the Mahavakya of the Sama Veda—"Tat Twam Asi—That Thou Art". In accordance with this view, the first six discourses deal with the path of action or Karma Yoga, that is, the nature of "Thou". It is called the Twam-pada. The next six discourses explain the path of devotion, the nature of "That". This is called the Tat-pada. The concluding six discourses treat of the path of knowledge, the nature of the middle term "Art". Hence, it is called the Asi-pada, which establishes the identity of the individual soul with the Supreme

Soul. The eighteen discourses are not woven in a discordant manner. Each one is intimately or vitally connected with its precedent. Arjuna became very despondent. Lord Krishna's opening remarks in the second discourse, which bespeak of the immortality of the soul, open his eyes and give him strength and courage. Arjuna then learns the technique of Karma Yoga and renunciation of the fruits of actions. He learns the methods of controlling the senses and the mind and practising concentration and meditation. This is followed by a description of the various manifestations of the Lord in order to prepare him for the vision of the Cosmic Form. Arjuna experiences the magnificent Cosmic Vision and understands the glorious nature of a liberated being. He is then given knowledge of the Field and the Knower of the Field, the three Gunas and the Purushottama. His knowledge is completed by an explanation of the divine attributes, the three kinds of faith and the essence of the Yoga of renunciation. Just as a student is coached in a university, Arjuna is coached by Krishna for the attainment of knowledge of the Self in the spiritual university. Arjuna had various kinds of doubts; Lord x Krishna cleared them one by one. He pushed Arjuna up the ladder of Yoga from one rung to the next. Eventually, Arjuna placed his foot on the highest rung, attained the supreme knowledge of the Self and exclaimed in joy: "O my Lord! my delusion has been destroyed. I have attained knowledge through Thy Grace. I am firm. All my doubts have now vanished in toto. I will act according to Thy word". You can become a liberated sage by annihilating the ego and the currents of likes and dislikes; by annihilating desires and cravings and destroying their residual potencies. Thus, you can rest in your true essential nature as Existence-Knowledge-Bliss Absolute and still be active in the affairs of the world. Now you will not be bound by your actions since the idea of doership has been destroyed by the attainment of knowledge of the Self. This is the keynote of the Gita. The Two Ways The seers of the Upanishads emphatically declare that the real man is the all-pervading, immortal Soul which is the substratum of this body, mind and world, which is behind the five sheaths, namely, the food, vital, mental, intellectual and bliss sheaths. The goal of life is to directly cognise or realise this self-luminous Self which is hidden in this body as fire is hidden in wood or as butter in milk. This Self is the inner ruler, the unseen governor or hidden proprietor of this house, the body. Real religion is the attainment of this transcendental, supreme, undying, undecaying Essence through constant and intense meditation. Real life is life in the eternal Soul. True life is identification with this Supreme Soul, which exists in the past, present and future, which has neither a beginning, middle nor end, which has neither parts nor limbs, which is neither subtle nor gross. The sages of ancient times attained this mysterious and most marvellous state through the eye of intuition or the divine third eye. They then explained the things of this world in the light of their intuitive knowledge of the Self. This is the direct method of Self-realisation. You can ascend the summit of the hill of knowledge through science, art, Nature, music, etc. This is the indirect method. From the effect you go to the cause and ultimately reach the causeless Cause or Para Brahman, the Truth which is transcendental. Our Western scientists will grope in utter darkness if their purpose is only to invent some things for our physical convenience. The goal of science is to discover the one ultimate Truth which is the substratum of the atoms, molecules, electrons, energy, motion and all physical and mental phenomena and laws of Nature by means of enquiry, observation, analysis, investigation and study of these laws in operation. A Vedantin is the real scientist. Only his mode of approach to the Truth is different. The scientist who in the past proclaimed that there was nothing beyond this world now proclaims: "The more I know of phenomena, the more I am puzzled. Intellect is finite and cold. Behind these changing phenomena there is the unchanging noumenon. Behind the dynamic rotating electrons, there is the static, motionless something, or something beyond the intellect and the world". xi Reconciliation of the Paths In the Vishnu Purana, Bhagavan Vishnu is highly eulogised and a secondary place is given to Lord Shiva. In the Shiva Purana, Lord Shiva is immensely praised whilst Lord Vishnu is secondary. In the Devi Bhagavatam, the Divine Mother is given prominence above Lord Shiva and Lord Vishnu. All this is done in order to create in the aspirant intense and unswerving faith in his favourite Deity. All Deities are one; they are different aspects of the Lord. It is simply absurd to believe that Shiva is inferior to Vishnu, or vice versa. In the same manner, in one place in the Gita, Lord Krishna praises Karma Yoga: "The Yoga of action is superior to the renunciation of action"—V.2. In another place He praises Raja Yoga: "The Yogi is thought to be superior to the ascetics and even superior to men of knowledge; he is also superior to men of action. Therefore, be thou a Yogi, O Arjuna!"—VI.46. In yet another place Lord Krishna praises the path of Bhakti Yoga: "The highest Purusha, O Arjuna, is attainable by unswerving devotion to Him alone within whom all beings dwell and by whom all this is pervaded!"—VIII.22. In one place He praises Jnana Yoga: "Noble indeed are all these; but I deem the wise man as My very Self; for, steadfast in mind, he is established in Me alone as the supreme goal"—VII.18. A beginner is confused when he comes across these seemingly contradictory verses. But, if you think deeply, there is no room for any confusion. Krishna praises each Yoga in order to create interest in the aspirant in his particular path. The Gita is a book for the people of the world at large. It was not meant for Arjuna alone. Each Yoga is as efficacious as the other. Essence of the Gita The Gita again and again emphasises that one should cultivate an attitude of non-attachment or detachment. It urges repeatedly that an individual should live in the world like water on a lotus leaf. "He who does actions, offering them to Brahman and abandoning attachment, is not tainted by sin as a lotus leaf by water"—V.10. Attachment is due to infatuation. It is the offspring of the quality of Rajas. Detachment is born of Sattwa. The former is a demoniacal attribute, the latter a divine one. Attachment is born of ignorance, selfishness and passion and brings with it death; detachment is wisdom and brings with it freedom. The practice of detachment is a rigorous discipline. You may stumble like a baby who is just learning to walk, but you will have to rise up again with a cheerful heart. Failures are not stumbling-blocks but steppingstones to success. Try to dwell always in your own Self. Abide in your centre. Think of the Self constantly. Then all attachments will die automatically. Attachment to the Lord is a potent antidote to annihilate all worldly attachments. He who has no attachments can really love others, for his love is pure and divine. "Therefore, without attachment do thou always perform action which should be done; for, by performing action without attachment man reaches the Supreme"—III.19. xii In Defence Some people study the Gita in order to find loopholes and criticise the teachings contained in it. The teachings of the Gita can only be understood if you approach it with a reverential attitude of mind and with intense faith. Recently someone wrote a criticism in the newspaper: "The Gita is not a sacred book at all. It teaches violence. Lord Krishna asked Arjuna to kill even his dear relations and preceptors". It is clear that this critic obviously has no real knowledge or understanding of the Gita. He is like Virochana who received spiritual instructions from Prajapati and took the body as being the Self on account of his perverted intellect. He is obviously a follower of the philosophy of the flesh. He cannot comprehend the depths of the Gita philosophy as his mind is callous and impervious to the reception of its truths. He has read the Gita not to gain spiritual knowledge but to attack it. The answer to his criticism lies in a proper understanding of the following verses: "He who takes the Self to be the slayer and he who thinks He is slain, neither of them knows. He slays not nor is He slain"—II.19; "Therefore, stand up and obtain fame. Conquer the enemies and enjoy the unrivalled kingdom. Verily by Me have they been already slain; be thou a mere instrument, O Arjuna!"—XI.33; "He who is free from the egoistic notion, whose intellect is untainted (by good or evil), though he slays these people, he slayeth not, nor is he bound (by the action)"—XVIII.17. Just as coloured dye stands out more clearly only when the original material is pure white, so also the instructions of a sage penetrate and settle down only in the hearts of aspirants whose minds are calm, who have no desire for enjoyments and whose impurities have been destroyed. For this reason an aspirant is expected to possess the qualifications of keen discrimination, dispassion, control of the mind and senses, and aversion to worldly attractions, before he can practise the threefold Sadhana of hearing the scriptures, reflecting upon them, and meditating upon their significance. Discipline and purification of the mind and the senses are the prerequisites for aspirants on the path of God-realisation. Even when the nature of God is explained, those who have not been purged of their faults and impurities would either disbelieve or misbelieve it, as was the case with Indra and Virochana. Therefore, knowledge as inculcated arises only in him who has purified himself by austerity, performed either in this or in a previous birth. The Upanishads declare: "To that high-souled man whose devotion to his preceptor is as great as that to the Lord, the secrets explained here become illumined". Some people catch fish in the Ganges river to satisfy their palate. Then they quote the Gita in support of their evil actions: "Weapons cut It not, fire burns It not, water wets It not, wind dries It not"—II.23. Wonderful philosophy indeed! Devils can also quote scriptures. These people are the followers of the Virochana school. They are evil-doing, deluded and the vilest of men. They cannot hope to understand the teachings of the Gita as their wisdom has been destroyed by illusion and they have embraced the nature of demons. May the Lord grant them a subtle and pure intellect, xiii inner spiritual strength and right understanding to comprehend the teachings of the Gita in their proper light and live in their spirit! Some ignorant people say: "Lord Krishna was not God. He was not an Avatara or Incarnation. He was a passionate cowherd who lustfully played with the Gopis". What was the age of Lord Krishna at that time? Was He not a boy of seven? Could there have been a tinge of passion in Him? Who can understand the secret of the Rasa Lila and Madhurya Bhava—the culmination of the highest state of devotion or total surrender to the Lord? It is only Narada, Sukadeva, Chaitanya, Mira, Ramananda and the Gopis who could understand the secret of the Rasa Lila. The Gopis only are qualified for this divine sport. Did He not play miracles when He was a boy? Did He not show that He was the Avatara of Lord Hari? Did He not show His Cosmic Form to His mother when He was only a baby? Did He not subdue the serpent, Kaliya, by standing on its hood? Did He not multiply Himself as countless Krishnas for the satisfaction of the Gopis? Who were the Gopis? Were they not God-intoxicated beings who saw Krishna alone everywhere, even in themselves? The sound of the flute would throw them in a state of ecstasy or holy communion. They were above body-consciousness. Just listen to the fate of such people who cavil and carp at the Lord: "The foolish think of Me, the Unmanifest, as having manifestation, knowing not My higher, immutable and most excellent form"—VII.24; "Fools disregard Me, clad in human form, not knowing My higher Being as the great Lord of all beings"; "Empty of hopes, of vain actions, of vain knowledge and senseless, they verily are possessed of the deceitful nature of demons and undivine beings"—IX.11-12; "These cruel haters—the worst among men in the world—I hurl these evil-doers into the womb of demons only"; "Entering into demoniacal wombs and deluded birth after birth, not attaining Me, they thus fall, O Arjuna, into a condition lower than that"-XVI.19-20. Some thoughtless people begin to entertain a doubt and say: "How could the Gita have been taught to Arjuna on the battlefield in such a short time? It could not." This is wrong. It was all a revelation to Arjuna. The Lord gave Arjuna the divine eye of intuition. He can do anything. His Grace can make the dumb man eloquent and the cripple a climber of mountains. Solutions to Conflicting Verses A critic says: "In the Gita, III.33, it is said, 'Even a wise man acts in accordance with his own nature; beings follow their nature; what can restraint do?' What then is the use of our attempt at controlling the senses and the mind when our nature is so powerful and overwhelming? How can our Sadhana overcome it?" In the very next verse, Lord Krishna distinctly advises us to control likes and dislikes. Our nature can be subdued by Sadhana. When studying the Gita you should not confine the meaning to one verse exclusively, but see its connection with the previous and succeeding verses of the same discourse as well as of all the other discourses. You have to frequently make cross references before you get the right answer. xiv Those who disregard the Lord's commandment: "Renouncing all actions in Me, with the mind centred in the Self free from hope and egoism and from mental fever, do thou fight", and who sit quiet, renouncing their own duty, will not derive any benefit by such renunciation. The power of Maya is invincible to even wise men; then how much more difficult it would be for worldly men to conquer it! For them, renunciation of work without attainment of knowledge is undesirable. They will be caught in the clutches of Maya. Of what avail is their effort to control the senses, or what can restraint do in their case? These worldly men cannot escape the clutches of likes and dislikes. Even the residual good tendencies in the wise men work in accordance with the qualities of their nature, namely, Sattwa, Rajas and Tamas. The wise too are affected by the three Gunas when they are not actually in the state of Samadhi. But they have no attachment to the body and other objects of enjoyment and, therefore, are not affected mentally. They are ever serene, self-contented and self-satisfied. They do not long for objects not attained nor weep over things lost. Another objector says: "In the Gita, XVIII.61, Lord Krishna says, 'The Lord dwells in the hearts of all beings, O Arjuna, causing all beings, by His illusive power, to revolve as if mounted on a machine!' Is man then a perfect slave? Is he like a straw tossed about here and there? Has he not any free will to act?" Krishna tries His best to persuade Arjuna to do his duty. He wants to extract work from him. So He speaks of Arjuna's utter helplessness. In VI.5, Krishna preaches about right exertion: "Let a man lift himself by his own Self alone, let him not lower himself; for this self is the friend of oneself and this self alone is the enemy of oneself". Being under the sway of one's nature, the natural duties can never be forsaken. One's duty should in no case be ignored. The Lord, the inner ruler, is the director of the individual soul. As long as one is not free from ignorance, one is bound to one's duty. Arjuna's duty as a Kshatriya was to fight; and Lord Krishna wanted him to do just that. The Lord has also said that "one's own duty is good". Yet another critic says: "In XV.7, the Lord says: 'An eternal portion of Myself, having become a living soul in the world of life, draws to itself the five senses with the mind for the sixth, abiding in Nature'. It is quite clear that the individual soul is a part of Brahman, the Absolute. How can we say that it is identical with Brahman? The doctrine of Advaita is therefore wrong". In VII.17, the Lord says: "Of them, the wise, ever steadfast and devoted to the One, excels; for I am exceedingly dear to the wise and he is dear to Me". Here He speaks of identity. The doctrine of non-dualism is quite correct. Non-dualism is the highest realisation. The Lord gives instructions according to the aspirant's qualification. Advaita philosophy can be grasped only by a microscopic few. So, He speaks of other philosophical doctrines in different places to suit different kinds of aspirants. From the absolute point of view there is neither the individual soul nor Self-realisation; Brahman alone exists. Dualism, qualified monism and pure monism are different rungs in the ladder of realisation. The truth is that the individual soul and Brahman are one in essence. All these schools eventually reach the Advaitic goal of oneness. Understand things in their proper light. xv Epilogue India is held in high esteem by the Westerners on account of the Gita. Gandhiji once visited one of the biggest libraries in London and asked the librarian which book was issued most frequently. The librarian said that it was the Gita. It is very popular throughout the world. All aspirants should try to get the whole eighteen discourses by heart. This can be achieved through daily study over a period of about one year at a rate of two verses a day. Study of the Gita must be made compulsory in all schools and colleges of India; nay, of the whole world. It must become a textbook for students of schools and colleges. It should find a very important place in every scheme of education. Only that system of education wherein moral and spiritual training are imparted along with secular knowledge can be deemed sound, practical, sensible and perfect. Hold the magnificent torch of faith. Float high the unique banner of peace. Wear the magnificent shield of dispassion. Put on the marvellous coat of arms of discrimination. Sing the immortal song of Soham, Shivoham, Radheshyam or Sitaram. March boldly with the band of Pranava. Blow the conch of courage. Kill the enemies of ignorance and egoism and enter the illimitable kingdom of God. My silent adorations to Lord Ganesh, Lord Subramanya, Lord Rama, Sita Devi, Sri Saraswathi, Sri Shankara, Bhagavan Vyasa, Sri Padmapadacharya, Sri Hastamalakacharya, Sri Totakacharya, Sri Sureshvaracharya, Sri Jnana Dev, Sri Swami Visvananda, Sri Swami Vishnudevananda, and all the Brahma Vidya Gurus and commentators on the Gita, through whose Grace and blessings alone I was able to write this commentary! May their blessings be upon you all! Glory, glory to the Gita! Glory to Lord Krishna, who placed the Gita before men of this world to attain liberation! May His blessings be upon you all! May the Gita be your centre, ideal and goal! Blessed is the man who studies the Gita daily! Twice blessed is he who lives in the spirit of the Gita! Thrice blessed is he who has realised the knowledge of the Gita or attained Self-knowledge! Om Tat Sat! Om Shanti, Shanti, Shanti!

Dhritarashtra and Pandu were brothers. Dhritarashtra married Gandhari, and Pandu was married to Kunti and Madri. King Pandu was cursed for a sin while hunting, due to which he was not permitted to unite with his wife. Kunti got a boon through her sincere service of a wise sage in her younger age, and she begot three children, namely, Yudhisthira, Bhima and Arjuna from Yama, Vayu and Indra respectively. Madri had twins, Nakula and Sahadeva, through the celestial physicians called Asvini-Devatas. Dhritarashtra had a hundred and one children by his wife Gandhari. Pandu passed away and his sons, the Pandavas, were all brought up by Dhritarashtra along with his sons known as Kauravas. The Pandavas and Kauravas grew up together, but due to the braveness and intelligence of the former, the Kauravas were unable to tolerate them. Hence the Pandavas decided to live separately, sharing half of their kingdom. The Pandavas' pomp, wealth and glory displayed during the Rajasuya Yajna aroused deep jealousy and greed in the mind of Duryodhana, the chief of the Kauravas, who, with the cunning advice of his uncle, Sakuni, invited Yudhisthira to a game of dice and fraudulently defeated him, whereby all his wealth and possessions, including Draupadi, were lost. Finally it was settled that the Pandavas, including Draupadi, should repair to the forest for twelve years in exile, after which they had to live incognito for another year, untraced by the Kauravas. During this period the kingdom was to be ruled by the wicked Duryodhana. Having successfully completed these thirteen years of exile, facing many obstacles and dangers instigated by the Kauravas, the Pandavas, as per the terms of the agreement, approached the Kauravas for their share of the kingdom. Duryodhana, however, flatly refused to part with as much land as could be covered by the point of a needle. According to the advice of Mother Kunti and with the inspiration of Lord Krishna, the Pandavas decided upon war and tried to establish their rightful claim on the kingdom by overcoming the Kauravas. Duryodhana and Arjuna, from the side of the Kauravas and Pandavas respectively, were sent to Dwaraka to seek the help of the Yadava hero, Lord Krishna, in the battle. They both found Krishna resting on a couch in His palace. Duryodhana went in and occupied a seat at the head of the couch while Arjuna stood near the feet of the Lord. The moment Sri Krishna opened His eyes, He naturally saw Arjuna first, and then Duryodhana sitting on a chair. After enquiry of their welfare and the purpose of their visit, Sri Krishna, according to the prevailing custom, gave the first choice to Arjuna, because of his age, and also because of His sight of Arjuna first. Krishna asked Arjuna to fulfil his desire by selecting

Him unarmed or His powerful army called Narayani Sena. Arjuna, who was a devotee of Sri Krishna, expressed his desire to have the Lord with him, neglecting the powerful Narayani Sena, even though Krishna warned that He would remain a witness, bound by the vow of not participating in battle and not taking up arms. Duryodhana, with great delight, thinking that Arjuna was foolish, expressed his wish for the powerful army to help his side in the battle. When Krishna asked Arjuna why he chose Him when He was not for taking up arms, Arjuna said, "O Lord! You have the power to destroy all the forces by a mere sight. Why then should I prefer that worthless army? I have for a long time been cherishing a desire in my heart that you should act as my charioteer. Kindly fulfil my desire in this war." xvii The Lord, who is ever the most devoted lover of His devotees, accepted his request with pleasure; and thus Krishna became the charioteer of Arjuna in the battle of the Mahabharata. After the return of Duryodhana and Arjuna from Dwaraka, Lord Krishna Himself went once to Hastinapura as the emissary of the Pandavas and tried to prevent the war. But then, under the guidance of Sakuni, the egoistic Duryodhana refused to agree to the peace mission and tried to imprison Lord Krishna, at which Krishna showed His Supreme Form (Viswarupa). Even the blind Dhritarashtra saw it by the Lord's Grace. King Dhritarashtra, due to his attachment to his sons, failed to control them, and the Kaurava chief, Duryodhana, with vain hope, decided to meet the powerful Pandavas in war. When both sides were prepared to commence the battle, the sage Veda Vyasa approached blind Dhritarashtra and said, "If you wish to see this terrible carnage with your own eyes I can give you the gift of vision." The Kaurava king replied, "O Chief of the Brahmarishis! I have no desire to see with my own eyes this slaughter of my family, but I should like to hear all the details of the battle." Then the sage conferred the gift of divine vision on Sanjaya, the trusty counsellor of the king, and told the king, "Sanjaya will describe to you all the incidents of the war. Whatever happens in the course of the war, he will directly see, hear or otherwise come to know. Whether an incident takes place before his eyes or behind his back, during the day or during the night, privately or in public, and whether it is reduced to actual action or appears only in thought, it will not remain hidden from his view. He will come to know everything, exactly as it happens. No weapon will touch his body nor will he feel tired." After the ten days of continued war between the Pandavas and the Kauravas, when the great warrior Bhishma was thrown down from his chariot by Arjuna, Sanjaya announces the news to Dhritarashtra. In agony the king asks Sanjaya to narrate the full details of the previous ten days war, from the very beginning, in all detail as it happened. Here commences the Bhagavad Gita.

CHAPTER TWO

PRAYER TO LORD KRISHNA

Krishnaaya vaasudevaaya devakeenandanaaya cha; Nandagopakumaaraaya govindaaya namo namah. I bow again and again to Lord Krishna, son of Vasudeva, the delighter of Devaki, the darling of Nandagopa, the protector of cows. O Krishna! Thou art my sweet companion now. Thou hast a soft corner for me in Thy heart. Teach me now the mysteries of Thy divine play and the secrets of Vedanta. Thou sayest in the Gita: "I am the author of Vedanta and the knower of the Vedas". Thou art my best teacher. Explain to me the intricate details of Vedanta. Give me easy lessons. Kindly explain; why did Sukadev, a Brahma Jnani who was always absorbed in Brahman, teach the Bhagavata to King Parikshit? What are the differences in the experiences of a Bhakta who enjoys union with God, of a Yogi who is established in the highest Superconscious State, and of a Jnani firmly established in the state of oneness or Brahman? What is the real difference between 1 liberation while living and disembodied liberation, between the transcendent state and the state beyond it, between the perishable Person, the imperishable Person and the Supreme Person? Let me be frank with Thee, O Krishna, because Thou art the indweller of my heart, the witness of my mind, and the Lord of my life-breath! I cannot hide anything from Thee, because Thou directly witnesseth all the thoughts that emanate from my mind. I have no fear of Thee. Thou art my friend now. Treat me like Arjuna. I shall sing and dance. You can play on the flute. Let us eat sugar-candy and butter together. Let us sing. Teach me the Gita. Let me hear it directly from Thy lips once more. O Thou invisible One! O adorable and Supreme One! Thou penetratest and permeatest this vast universe from the unlimited space down to the tiny blade of grass at my feet. Thou art the basis of all names and forms. Thou art the apple of my eye, the divine love of my heart, the life of my life, the very soul of my soul, the illuminator of my intellect and senses, the sweet mystic music of my heart, and the substance of my physical, mental and causal bodies. I recognise Thee alone as the mighty ruler of this universe and the inner controller of my three bodies. I prostrate again and again before Thee, my Lord. Thou art my sole refuge. I trust Thee alone, O ocean of mercy and love! Elevate, enlighten, guide and protect me. Remove the obstacles on my spiritual path. Remove the veil of ignorance. O Thou supreme world-teacher! I cannot bear any longer, even for a second, the miseries of this physical body, this life and this worldly existence. Meet me quickly, O Prabhu! I am pining, I am melting. Listen, listen, listen to my fervent, innermost prayer. Do not be cruel, my Lord. Thou art the friend of the afflicted. Thou art one who raises the downtrodden. Thou art the purifier of the fallen. O magnificent Lord of love and compassion! O fountain-head of bliss and knowledge! Thou art the eye of our eye, the ear of our ear, the breath of our breath, the mind of our mind, the soul of our soul. Thou art the unseen seer, the unthought thinker, the unheard hearer, the unknown knower. Pray, deliver us from temptation. Give us light, knowledge and purity. O Lord of my breath! O all-pervading Lord of the universe, accept my humble prayer! Guide me. Lift me from the mire of worldliness. Enlighten me. Protect me. Thee alone I adore; Thee alone I worship; on Thee alone I meditate in Thee alone I take sole refuge.

CHAPTER THREE

GITA MAHATMYA GLORY OF THE GITA

Sri Ganeshaaya Namah! Gopaalakrishnaaya Namah! Dharovaacha: Bhagavan parameshaana bhaktiravyabhichaarinee; Praarabdham bhujyamaanasya katham bhavati he prabho. The Earth said: 1. O Bhagavan, the Supreme Lord! How can unflinching devotion arise in him who is immersed in his Prarabdha Karmas (worldly life), O Lord? Sri Vishnuruvaacha: Praarabdham bhujyamaano hi geetaabhyaasaratah sadaa; Sa muktah sa sukhee loke karmanaa nopalipyate. Lord Vishnu said: 2. Though engaged in the performance of worldly duties, one who is regular in the study of the Gita becomes free. He is the happy man in this world. He is not bound by Karma. Mahaapaapaadipaapaani geetaadhyaanam karoti chet; Kwachit sparsham na kurvanti nalineedalam ambuvat. 3. Just as the water stains not the lotus leaf, even so sins do not taint him who is regular in the recitation of the Gita. Geetaayaah pustakam yatra yatra paathah pravartate; Tatra sarvaani teerthaani prayaagaadeeni tatra vai. 4. All the sacred centres of pilgrimage, like Prayag and other places, dwell in that place where the Gita is kept, and where the Gita is read. Sarve devaashcha rishayo yoginahpannagaashcha ye; Gopaalaa gopikaa vaapi naaradoddhava paarshadaih. 5. All the gods, sages, Yogins, divine serpents, Gopalas, Gopikas (friends and devotees of Lord Krishna), Narada, Uddhava and others (dwell here). Sahaayo jaayate sheeghram yatra geetaa pravartate; Yatra geetaavichaarashcha pathanam paathanam shrutam; Tatraaham nishchitam prithvi nivasaami sadaiva hi. 3 BHAGAVAD GITA 6. Help comes quickly where the Gita is recited and, O Earth, I ever dwell where it is read, heard, taught and contemplated upon! Geetaashraye'ham tishthaami geetaa me chottamam griham; Geetaajnaanam upaashritya treen Uokaan paalayaamyaham. 7. I take refuge in the Gita, and the Gita is My best abode. I protect the three worlds with the knowledge of the Gita. Geetaa me paramaa vidyaa brahmaroopaa na samshayah; Ardhamaatraaksharaa nityaa swaanirvaachyapadaatmikaa. 8. The Gita is My highest science, which is doubtless of the form of Brahman, the Eternal, the Ardhamatra (of the Pranava Om), the ineffable splendour of the Self. Chidaanandena krishnena proktaa swamukhato'rjuna; Vedatrayee paraanandaa tatwaarthajnaanasamyutaa. 9. It was spoken by the blessed Lord Krishna, the all-knowing, through His own mouth, to Arjuna. It contains the essence of the Vedas—the knowledge of the Reality. It is full of supreme bliss. COMMENTARY: The Gita contains the cream of the Vedas and Upanishads. Hence it is a universal scripture suited for people of all temperaments and for all ages. Yoashtaadasha japen nityam naro nishchalamaanasah; Jnaanasiddhim sa labhate tato yaati param padam. 10. He who recites the eighteen chapters of the Bhagavad Gita daily, with a pure and unshaken mind, attains perfection in knowledge, and reaches the highest state or supreme goal. Paathe'asamarthah sampoornam tato'rdham paathamaacharet; Tadaa godaanajam punyam labhate naatra samshayah. 11. If a complete reading is not possible, even if only half is read, he attains the benefit of giving a cow as a gift. There is no doubt about this. Tribhaagam pathamaanastu gangaasnaanaphalam labhet; Shadamsham japamaanastu somayaagaphalam labhet. 12. He who recites one-third part of it achieves the merit of a bath in the sacred river Ganges; and who recites one-sixth of it attains the merit of performing a Soma sacrifice (a kind of ritual). Ekaadhyaayam tu yo nityam pathate bhaktisamyutah; Rudralokam avaapnoti gano bhootwaa vasecchiram. 4 GITA MAHATMYA 13. That person who reads one discourse with supreme faith and devotion attains to the world of Rudra and, having become a Gana (an attendant of Lord Shiva), lives there for many years. Adhyaayam shlokapaadam vaa nityam yah pathate narah; Sa yaati narataam yaavanmanwantaram vasundhare. 14. If one reads a discourse or even a part of a verse daily he, O Earth, retains a human body till the end of a Manvantara (71 Mahayugas or 308,448,000 years). Geetaayaah shloka dashakam sapta pancha chatushtayam; Dwautreenekam tadardhamvaa shlokaanaam yah pathennarah. Chandralokam avaapnoti varshaanaam ayutam dhruvam; Geetaapaathasamaayukto mrito maanushataam vrajet. 15-16. He who repeats ten, seven, five, four, three, two verses or even one or half of it, attains the region of the moon and lives there for 10,000 years. Accustomed to the daily study of the Gita, a dying man comes back to life again as a human being. Geetaabhyaasam punah kritwaa labhate muktim uttamaam; Geetetyucchaarasamyukto mriyamaano gatim labhet. 17. By repeated study of the Gita, he attains liberation. Uttering the word Gita at the time of death, a person attains liberation. Geetaarthashravanaasakto mahaapaapayuto'pi vaa; Vaikuntham samavaapnoti vishnunaa saha modate. 18. Though full of sins, one who is ever intent on hearing the meaning of the Gita, goes to the kingdom of God and rejoices with Lord Vishnu. Geetaartham dhyaayate nityam kritwaa karmaani bhoorishah; Jeevanmuktah sa vijneyo dehaante paramam padam. 19. He who meditates on the meaning of the Gita, having performed many virtuous actions, attains the supreme goal after death. Such an individual should be considered a true Jivanmukta. COMMENTARY: A Jivanmukta is one who has attained liberation while living. Geetaam aashritya bahavo bhoobhujo janakaadayah; Nirdhootakalmashaa loke geetaa yaataah param padam. 20. In this world, taking refuge in the Gita, many kings like Janaka and others reached the highest state or goal, purified of all sins. Geetaayaah pathanam kritwaa maahaatmyam naiva yah pathet; Vrithaa paatho bhavet tasya shrama eva hyudaahritah. 5 BHAGAVAD GITA 21. He who fails to read this "Glory of the Gita" after having read the Gita, loses the benefit thereby, and the effort alone remains. COMMENTARY: This is to test and confirm the faith of the reader in the Bhagavad Gita, which is not a mere philosophical book but the word of God and should therefore be studied with great faith and devotion. The Gita Mahatmya generates this devotion in one's heart. Etanmaahaatmyasamyuktam geetaabhyaasam karoti yah; Sa tatphalamavaapnoti durlabhaam gatim aapnuyaat. 22. One who studies the Gita, together with this "Glory of the Gita", attains the fruits mentioned above, and reaches the state which is otherwise very difficult to be attained. Suta Uvaacha: Maahaatmyam etad geetaayaah mayaa proktam sanaatanam; Geetaante cha pathedyastu yaduktam tatphalam labhet. Suta said: 23. This greatness or "Glory of the Gita", which is eternal, as narrated by me, should be read at the end of the study of the Gita, and the fruits mentioned therein will be obtained. Iti srivaraahapuraane srigeetaamaahaatmyam sampoornam. Thus ends the "Glory of the Gita" contained in the Varaha Purana.

CHAPTER FOUR

GITA DHYANAM

Om paarthaaya pratibodhitaam bhagavataa naaraayanenaswayam, Vyaasena grathitaam puraanamuninaa madhye mahaabhaaratam; Advaitaamritavarshineem bhagavateem ashtaadashaa dhyaayineem, Amba twaam anusandadhaami bhagavadgeete bhavadweshineem. 1. Om. O Bhagavad Gita, with which Partha was illumined by Lord Narayana Himself, and which was composed within the Mahabharata by the ancient sage, Vyasa, O Divine Mother, the destroyer of rebirth, the showerer of the nectar of Advaita, and consisting of eighteen discourses—upon Thee, O Gita, O affectionate Mother, I meditate! Namostu te vyaasa vishaalabuddhe phullaaravindaayatapatranetra; Yena twayaa bhaaratatailapoornah prajwaalito jnaanamayah pradeepah. 2. Salutations unto thee, O Vyasa, of broad intellect and with eyes like the petals of a full-blown lotus, by whom the lamp of knowledge, filled with the oil of the Mahabharata, has been lighted! Prapannapaarijaataaya totravetraikapaanaye; Jnaanamudraaya krishnaaya geetaamritaduhe namah. 3. Salutations to Lord Krishna, the Parijata or the Kalpataru or the bestower of all desires for those who take refuge in Him, the holder of the whip in one hand, the holder of the symbol of divine knowledge and the milker of the divine nectar of the Bhagavad Gita! Sarvopanishado gaavo dogdhaa gopaalanandanah; Paartho vatsah sudheer bhoktaa dugdham geetaamritam mahat. 4. All the Upanishads are the cows; the milker is Krishna; the cowherd boy, Partha (Arjuna), is the calf; men of purified intellect are the drinkers; the milk is the great nectar of the Gita. Vasudevasutam devam kamsachaanooramardanam; Devakeeparamaanandam krishnam vande jagadgurum. 5. I salute Sri Krishna, the world-teacher, son of Vasudeva, the destroyer of Kamsa and Chanura, the supreme bliss of Devaki! Bheeshmadronatataa jayadrathajalaa gaandhaaraneelotpalaa; Shalyagraahavatee kripena vahanee karnena velaakulaa; Ashwatthaamavikarna-ghora-makaraa duryodhanaavartinee; Sotteernaa khalu paandavai rananadee kaivartakah keshavah. 7 BHAGAVAD GITA 6. With Kesava as the helmsman, verily was crossed by the Pandavas the battle-river, whose banks were Bhishma and Drona, whose water was Jayadratha, whose blue lotus was the king of Gandhara, whose crocodile was Salya, whose current was Kripa, whose billow was Karna, whose terrible alligators were Vikarna and Asvatthama, whose whirlpool was Duryodhana. Paaraasharya vachah sarojamamalam geetaarthagandhotkatam; Naanaakhyaanakakesaram harikathaa sambodhanaabodhitam; Loke sajjana shatpadairaharahah pepeeyamaanam mudaa; Bhooyaadbhaaratapankajam kalimala pradhwamsinah shreyase. 7. May this lotus of the Mahabharata, born in the lake of the words of Vyasa, sweet with the fragrance of the meaning of the Gita, with many stories as its stamens, fully opened by the discourses of Hari, the destroyer of the sins of Kali, and drunk joyously by the bees of good men in the world, become day by day the bestower of good to us! Mookam karoti vaachaalam pangum langhayate girim; Yatkripaa tamaham vande paramaanandamaadhavam. 8. I salute that Madhava, the source of supreme bliss, whose Grace makes the dumb eloquent and the cripple cross mountains! Yam brahmaa varunendrarudramarutah stunwanti divyaih stavaih, Vedaih saangapadakramopanishadair gaayanti yam saamagaah, Dhyaanaavasthitatadgatena manasaa pashyanti yam yogino, Yasyaantam na viduh suraasuraganaa devaaya tasmai namah. 9. Salutations to that God whom Brahma, Indra, Varuna, Rudra and the Maruts praise with divine hymns, of whom the Sama-chanters sing by the Vedas and their Angas (in the Pada and Krama methods), and by the Upanishads; whom the Yogis see with their minds absorbed in Him through meditation, and whose ends the hosts of Devas and Asuras know not!

CHAPTER FIVE

THE YOGA OF THE DESPONDENCY OF ARJUNA

The great Mahabharata war between the Pandavas and the Kauravas took place on the holy plain of Kurukshetra. After the failure of Lord Krishna's peace mission, when He Himself went to Hastinapura as the emissary of the Pandavas, there was no other alternative for the Pandavas but to engage in war for their rightful share of the kingdom. All the famous warriors from both sides had assembled on the battlefield. Tents and wagons, weapons and machines, chariots and animals covered the vast plain. Lord Krishna arrived on the scene in a magnificent chariot yoked by white horses. He was to act as the charioteer of Arjuna, one of the Pandava princes. The din of hundreds of conches, blaring forth suddenly, announced the commencement of the battle. Arjuna blew his conch "Devadatta", while Bhima, his brother, sounded the "Paundra". All the other great warriors blew their respective conches. As the two armies were arrayed, ready for battle, Arjuna requested Krishna to place his chariot between them so that he might survey his opponents. He was bewildered by the scene before him, for he beheld on both sides, fathers and grandfathers, teachers and uncles, fathers-in-law, grandsons, relatives and comrades. Confusion reigned in Arjuna's mind. Should he participate in this terrible carnage? Was it proper to destroy one's relatives for the sake of a kingdom and some pleasures? Would it not be much better for him to surrender everything in favour of his enemies and retire in peace? As these thoughts rushed into his mind, a feeling of despondency overtook Arjuna. He had no enthusiasm to engage in this battle. Letting his bow slip from his hands, Arjuna could do nothing but turn to Lord Krishna for guidance and enlightenment. Dhritaraashtra Uvaacha: Dharmakshetre kurukshetre samavetaa yuyutsavah; Maamakaah paandavaashchaiva kim akurvata sanjaya. Dhritarashtra said: 1. What did the sons of Pandu and also my people do when they had assembled together, eager for battle on the holy plain of Kurukshetra, O Sanjaya? Sanjaya Uvaacha: Drishtwaa tu paandavaaneekam vyudham duryodhanastadaa; 9 BHAGAVAD GITA Aachaaryam upasamgamya raajaa vachanam abraveet. Sanjaya said: 2. Having seen the army of the Pandavas drawn up in battle array, King Duryodhana then approached his teacher (Drona) and spoke these words: Pashyaitaam paanduputraanaam aachaarya mahateem chamoom; Vyoodhaam drupadaputrena tava shishyena dheemataa. 3. "Behold, O Teacher, this mighty army of the sons of Pandu, arrayed by the son of Drupada, thy wise disciple! Atra shooraa maheshwaasaa bheemaarjunasamaa yudhi; Yuyudhaano viraatashcha drupadashcha mahaarathah. 4. "Here are heroes, mighty archers, equal in battle to Bhima and Arjuna, Yuyudhana, Virata and Drupada, of the great car (mighty warriors), Dhrishtaketush chekitaanah kaashiraajashcha veeryavaan; Purujit kuntibhojashcha shaibyashcha narapungavah. 5. "Drishtaketu, Chekitana and the valiant king of Kasi, Purujit, and Kuntibhoja and Saibya, the best of men, Yudhaamanyushcha vikraanta uttamaujaashcha veeryavaan; Saubhadro draupadeyaashcha sarva eva mahaarathaah. 6. "The strong Yudhamanyu and the brave Uttamaujas, the son of Subhadra (Abhimanyu, the son of Arjuna), and the sons of Draupadi, all of great chariots (great heroes). Asmaakam tu vishishtaa ye taan nibodha dwijottama; Naayakaah mama sainyasya samjnaartham taan braveemi te. 7. "Know also, O best among the twice-born, the names of those who are the most distinguished amongst ourselves, the leaders of my army! These I name to thee for thy information. Bhavaan bheeshmashcha karnashcha kripashcha samitinjayah; Ashwatthaamaa vikarnashcha saumadattis tathaiva cha. 8. "Thyself and Bhishma, and Karna and Kripa, the victorious in war; Asvatthama, Vikarna, and Jayadratha, the son of Somadatta. Anye cha bahavah shooraa madarthe tyaktajeevitaah; Naanaashastrapraharanaah sarve yuddhavishaaradaah. 10 THE YOGA OF THE DESPONDENCY OF ARJUNA 9. "And also many other heroes who have given up their lives for my sake, armed with various weapons and missiles, all well skilled in battle. Aparyaaptam tad asmaakam balam bheeshmaabhirakshitam; Paryaaptam twidam eteshaam balam bheemaabhirakshitam. 10. "This army of ours marshalled by Bhishma is insufficient, whereas their army, marshalled by Bhima, is sufficient. Ayaneshu cha sarveshu yathaabhaagam avasthitaah; Bheeshmam evaabhirakshantu bhavantah sarva eva hi. 11. "Therefore, do ye all, stationed in your respective positions in the several divisions of the army, protect Bhishma alone". Tasya sanjanayan harsham kuruvriddhah pitaamahah; Simhanaadam vinadyocchaih shankham dadhmau prataapavaan. 12. His glorious grandsire (Bhishma), the eldest of the Kauravas, in order to cheer Duryodhana, now roared like a lion and blew his conch. Tatah shankhaashcha bheryashcha panavaanakagomukhaah; Sahasaivaabhyahanyanta sa shabdastumulo'bhavat. 13. Then (following Bhishma), conches and kettle-drums, tabors, drums and cow-horns blared forth quite suddenly (from the side of the Kauravas); and the sound was tremendous. Tatah shvetair hayair yukte mahati syandane sthitau; Maadhavah paandavashchaiva divyau shankhau pradadhmatuh. 14. Then also, Madhava (Krishna), and the son of Pandu (Arjuna), seated in their magnificent chariot yoked with white horses, blew their divine conches. Paanchajanyam hrisheekesho devadattam dhananjayah; Paundram dadhmau mahaashankham bheemakarmaa vrikodarah. 15. Hrishikesa blew the "Panchajanya" and Arjuna blew the "Devadatta", and Bhima, the doer of terrible deeds, blew the great conch, "Paundra". Anantavijayam raajaa kunteeputro yudhishthirah; Nakulah sahadevashcha sughoshamanipushpakau. 16. Yudhisthira, the son of Kunti, blew the "Anantavijaya"; and Sahadeva and Nakula blew the "Manipushpaka" and "Sughosha" conches. Kaashyashcha parameshwaasah shikhandee cha mahaarathah; 11 BHAGAVAD GITA Dhrishtadyumno viraatashcha saatyakishchaaparaajitah. 17. The king of Kasi, an excellent archer, Sikhandi, the mighty car-warrior, Dhristadyumna and Virata and Satyaki, the unconquered, Drupado draupadeyaashcha sarvashah prithiveepate; Saubhadrashcha mahaabaahuh shankhaan dadhmuh prithak prithak. 18. Drupada and the sons of Draupadi, O Lord of the Earth, and the son of Subhadra, the mighty-armed, all blew their respective conches! Sa ghosho dhaartaraashtraanaam hridayaani vyadaarayat; Nabhashcha prithiveem chaiva tumulo vyanunaadayan. 19. The tumultuous sound rent the hearts of Dhritarashtra's party, making both heaven and earth resound. Atha vyavasthitaan drishtwaa dhaartaraashtraan kapidhwajah; Pravritte shastrasampaate dhanurudyamya paandavah. Hrisheekesham tadaa vaakyamidamaaha maheepate; 20. Then, seeing all the people of Dhritarashtra's party standing arrayed and the discharge of weapons about to begin, Arjuna, the son of Pandu, whose ensign was that of a monkey, took up his bow and said the following to Krishna, O Lord of the Earth! Arjuna Uvaacha: Senayor ubhayormadhye ratham sthaapaya me'chyuta. Yaavad etaan nireekshe'ham yoddhukaamaan avasthitaan; Kair mayaa saha yoddhavyam asmin ranasamudyame. Arjuna said: 21-22. In the middle of the two armies, place my chariot, O Krishna, so that I may behold those who stand here, desirous to fight, and know with whom I must fight when the battle begins. Yotsyamaanaan avekshe'ham ya ete'tra samaagataah; Dhaartaraashtrasya durbuddher yuddhe priyachikeershavah. 23. For I desire to observe those who are assembled here to fight, wishing to please in battle Duryodhana, the evil-minded. Sanjaya Uvaacha: Evamukto hrisheekesho gudaakeshena bhaarata; Senayor ubhayormadhye sthaapayitwaa rathottamam. Sanjaya said: 12 THE YOGA OF THE DESPONDENCY OF ARJUNA 24. Being thus addressed by Arjuna, Lord Krishna, having stationed that best of chariots, O Dhritarashtra, in the midst of the two armies, Bheeshmadronapramukhatah sarveshaam cha maheekshitaam; Uvaacha paartha pashyaitaan samavetaan kuroon iti. 25. In front of Bhishma and Drona and all the rulers of the earth, said: "O Arjuna, behold now all these Kurus gathered together!" Tatraapashyat sthitaan paarthah pitrin atha pitaamahaan; Aachaaryaan maatulaan bhraatrun putraan pautraan sakheemstathaa. 26. Then Arjuna beheld there stationed, grandfathers and fathers, teachers, maternal uncles, brothers, sons, grandsons and friends, too. Shvashuraan suhridashchaiva senayorubhayorapi; Taan sameekshya sa kaunteyah sarvaan bandhoon avasthitaan. Kripayaa parayaa'vishto visheedannidam abraveet; 27. (He saw) fathers-in-law and friends also in both armies. The son of Kunti—Arjuna—seeing all these kinsmen standing arrayed, spoke thus sorrowfully, filled with deep pity. Arjuna Uvaacha: Drishtwemam swajanam krishna yuyutsum samupasthitam. Arjuna said: 28. Seeing these, my kinsmen, O Krishna, arrayed, eager to fight, Seedanti mama gaatraani mukham cha parishushyati; Vepathushcha shareere me romaharshashcha jaayate. 29. My limbs fail and my mouth is parched up, my body quivers and my hairs stand on end! Gaandeevam sramsate hastaat twak chaiva paridahyate; Na cha shaknomyavasthaatum bhramateeva cha me manah. 30. The (bow) "Gandiva" slips from my hand and my skin burns all over; I am unable even to stand, my mind is reeling, as it were. Nimittaani cha pashyaami vipareetaani keshava; Na cha shreyo'nupashyaami hatwaa swajanam aahave. 31. And I see adverse omens, O Kesava! I do not see any good in killing my kinsmen in battle. 13 BHAGAVAD GITA Na kaangkshe vijayam krishna na cha raajyam sukhaani cha; Kim no raajyena govinda kim bhogair jeevitena vaa. 32. For I desire neither victory, O Krishna, nor pleasures nor kingdoms! Of what avail is a dominion to us, O Krishna, or pleasures or even life? Yeshaam arthe kaangkshitam no raajyam bhogaah sukhaani cha; Ta ime'vasthitaa yuddhe praanaamstyaktwaa dhanaani cha. 33. Those for whose sake we desire kingdoms, enjoyments and pleasures, stand here in battle, having renounced life and wealth. Aachaaryaah pitarah putraastathaiva cha pitaamahaah; Maatulaah shwashuraah pautraah shyaalaah sambandhinas tathaa. 34. Teachers, fathers, sons and also grandfathers, grandsons, fathers-in-law, maternal uncles, brothers-in-law and relatives,— Etaan na hantum icchaami ghnato'pi madhusoodana; Api trailokya raajyasya hetoh kim nu maheekrite. 35. These I do not wish to kill, though they kill me, O Krishna, even for the sake of dominion over the three worlds, leave alone killing them for the sake of the earth! Nihatya dhaartaraashtraan nah kaa preetih syaaj janaardana; Paapam evaashrayed asmaan hatwaitaan aatataayinah. 36. By killing these sons of Dhritarashtra, what pleasure can be ours, O Janardana? Only sin will accrue by killing these felons. Tasmaan naarhaa vayam hantum dhaartaraashtraan swabaandhavaan; Swajanam hi katham hatwaa sukhinah syaama maadhava. 37. Therefore, we should not kill the sons of Dhritarashtra, our relatives; for, how can we be happy by killing our own people, O Madhava (Krishna)? Yadyapyete na pashyanti lobhopahatachetasah; Kulakshayakritam dosham mitradrohe cha paatakam. 38. Though they, with intelligence overpowered by greed, see no evil in the destruction of families, and no sin in hostility to friends, Katham na jneyam asmaabhih paapaad asmaan nivartitum; Kulakshayakritam dosham prapashyadbhir janaardana. 14 THE YOGA OF THE DESPONDENCY OF ARJUNA 39. Why should not we, who clearly see evil in the destruction of a family, learn to turn away from this sin, O Janardana (Krishna)? COMMENTARY: Ignorance of the law is no excuse and wanton sinful conduct is a crime unworthy of knowledgeable people. Kulakshaye pranashyanti kuladharmaah sanaatanaah; Dharme nashte kulam kritsnam adharmo'bhibhavatyuta. 40. In the destruction of a family, the immemorial religious rites of that family perish; on the destruction of spirituality, impiety overcomes the whole family. COMMENTARY: Dharma pertains to the duties and ceremonies practised by the family in accordance with scriptural injunctions. Adharmaabhibhavaat krishna pradushyanti kulastriyah; Streeshu dushtaasu vaarshneya jaayate varnasankarah. 41. By prevalence of impiety, O Krishna, the women of the family become corrupt and, women becoming corrupted, O Varsneya (descendant of Vrishni), there arises intermingling of castes! Sankaro narakaayaiva kulaghnaanaam kulasya cha; Patanti pitaro hyeshaam luptapindodakakriyaah. 42. Confusion of castes leads to hell the slayers of the family, for their forefathers fall, deprived of the offerings of rice-ball and water. Doshair etaih kulaghnaanaam varnasankarakaarakaih; Utsaadyante jaatidharmaah kuladharmaashcha shaashwataah. 43. By these evil deeds of the destroyers of the family, which cause confusion of castes, the eternal religious rites of the caste and the family are destroyed. Utsannakuladharmaanaam manushyaanaam janaardana; Narake'niyatam vaaso bhavateetyanushushruma. 44. We have heard, O Janardana, that inevitable is the dwelling for an unknown period in hell for those men in whose families the religious practices have been destroyed! Aho bata mahat paapam kartum vyavasitaa vayam; Yadraajya sukhalobhena hantum swajanam udyataah. 45. Alas! We are involved in a great sin in that we are prepared to kill our kinsmen through greed for the pleasures of a kingdom. 15 BHAGAVAD GITA Yadi maam aprateekaaram ashastram shastrapaanayah; Dhaartaraashtraa rane hanyus tanme kshemataram bhavet. 46. If the sons of Dhritarashtra, with weapons in hand, should slay me in battle, unresisting and unarmed, that would be better for me. Sanjaya Uvaacha: Evamuktwaa'rjunah sankhye rathopastha upaavishat; Visrijya sasharam chaapam shokasamvignamaanasah. Sanjaya said: 47. Having thus spoken in the midst of the battlefield, Arjuna, casting away his bow and arrow, sat down on the seat of the chariot with his mind overwhelmed with sorrow. Hari Om Tat Sat Iti Srimad Bhagavadgeetaasoopanishatsu Brahmavidyaayaam Yogashaastre Sri Krishnaarjunasamvaade Arjunavishaadayogo Naama Prathamo'dhyaayah. Thus in the Upanishads of the glorious Bhagavad Gita, the science of the Eternal, the scripture of Yoga, the dialogue between Sri Krishna and Arjuna, ends the first discourse entitled: "The Yoga Of the Despondency of Arjuna"

CHAPTER SIX

SANKHYA YOGA

Sanjaya explains the condition of Arjuna, who was agitated due to attachment and fear. Lord Krishna rebukes him for his dejection, which was due to Moha or attachment, and exhorts him to fight. After failing to convince Sri Krishna through his seemingly wise thoughts, Arjuna realises his helplessness and surrenders himself completely to the Lord, seeking His guidance to get over the conflict of his mind. The Lord takes pity on him and proceeds to enlighten him by various means. He explains to Arjuna the imperishable nature of the Atman, for which there is no past, present and future. The Atman never dies, therefore Arjuna should not grieve. As It transcends the five elements, namely, earth, water, fire, air and ether, It cannot be cut, burnt or dried. It is unchanging and eternal. Everyone experiences conditions like pleasure and pain, heat and cold, due to contact of objects with the senses. The senses carry the sensations through the nerves to the mind. One should 16 THE YOGA OF THE DESPONDENCY OF ARJUNA be able to withdraw the senses from objects, like the tortoise which withdraws all its limbs within. Krishna asserts that only one who has the capacity to be balanced in pleasure and pain alike is fit for immortality. Krishna goes on to tell Arjuna that if he refuses to fight and flees from the battle, people will be justified in condemning such action as unworthy of a warrior. Having taught Arjuna the immortal nature of the Atman, Lord Krishna turns to the performance of action without expectation of fruit. A man should not concern himself about the fruit of the action, like gain and loss, victory and defeat. These are in the hands of the Lord. He should perform all action with a balanced mind, calmly enduring the pairs of opposites like heat and cold, pleasure and pain, that inevitably manifest during action. Krishna advises Arjuna to fight, free from desire for acquisition of kingdom or preservation of it. Arjuna is eager to know the characteristics of a man who has a stable mind. Such a person, Krishna tells him, will have no desires at all. Since he is content within, having realised the Self, he is entirely free from desires. The consciousness of the Atman and abandonment of desires are simultaneous experiences. The various qualities of a Sthitaprajna (a stable-minded person) are described by the Lord. He will not be affected by adversity and will have no fear or anger. He will take things as they come, and will not have any likes and dislikes. He will neither hug the world nor hate it. The man of stable mind will have perfect control of the senses. The senses are powerful and draw the mind outwards. One should therefore turn one's gaze within and realise God who resides in the heart. The Yogi, having achieved a stable mind, remains steadfast even though all sense-objects come to him. He is unmoved and lives a life of eternal peace. Krishna concludes that the eternal Brahmic state frees one from delusion forever. Even at the end of life, when one departs from this body, one does not lose consciousness of one's identity with Brahman. Sanjaya Uvaacha: Tam tathaa kripayaavishtam ashrupoornaakulekshanam; Visheedantam idam vaakyam uvaacha madhusoodanah. Sanjaya said: 1. To him who was thus overcome with pity and who was despondent, with eyes full of tears and agitated, Krishna or Madhusudana (the destroyer of Madhu), spoke these words. Sri Bhagavaan Uvaacha: Kutastwaa kashmalam idam vishame samupasthitam; Anaaryajushtam aswargyam akeertikaram arjuna. 17 BHAGAVAD GITA The Blessed Lord said: 2. Whence is this perilous strait come upon thee, this dejection which is unworthy of thee, disgraceful, and which will close the gates of heaven upon thee, O Arjuna? Klaibyam maa sma gamah paartha naitat twayyupapadyate; Kshudram hridaya daurbalyam tyaktwottishtha parantapa. 3. Yield not to impotence, O Arjuna, son of Pritha! It does not befit thee. Cast off this mean weakness of the heart. Stand up, O scorcher of foes! Arjuna Uvaacha: Katham bheeshmamaham sankhye dronam cha madhusoodana; Ishubhih pratiyotsyaami poojaarhaavarisoodana. Arjuna said: 4. How, O Madhusudana, shall I fight in battle with arrows against Bhishma and Drona, who are fit to be worshipped, O destroyer of enemies? Guroon ahatwaa hi mahaanubhaavaan Shreyo bhoktum bhaikshyam apeeha loke; Hatwaarthakaamaamstu guroon ihaiva Bhunjeeya bhogaan rudhirapradigdhaan. 5. Better it is, indeed, in this world to accept alms than to slay the most noble teachers. But if I kill them, even in this world all my enjoyments of wealth and desires will be stained with (their) blood. Na chaitad vidmah kataran no gareeyo Yadwaa jayema yadi vaa no jayeyuh; Yaan eva hatwaa na jijeevishaamas Te'vasthitaah pramukhe dhaartaraashtraah. 6. I can hardly tell which will be better: that we should conquer them or they should conquer us. Even the sons of Dhritarashtra, after slaying whom we do not wish to live, stand facing us. Kaarpanyadoshopahataswabhaavah Pricchaami twaam dharmasammoodha chetaah; Yacchreyah syaan nishchitam broohi tanme Shishyaste'ham shaadhi maam twaam prapannam. 7. My heart is overpowered by the taint of pity, my mind is confused as to duty. I ask Thee: tell me decisively what is good for me. I am Thy disciple. Instruct me who has taken refuge in Thee. Na hi prapashyaami mamaapanudyaad 18 SANKHYA YOGA Yacchokam ucchoshanam indriyaanaam; Avaapya bhoomaavasapatnam riddham Raajyam suraanaam api chaadhipatyam. 8. I do not see that it would remove this sorrow that burns up my senses even if I should attain prosperous and unrivalled dominion on earth or lordship over the gods. Sanjaya Uvaacha: Evam uktwaa hrisheekesham gudaakeshah parantapah; Na yotsya iti govindam uktwaa tooshneem babhoova ha. Sanjaya said: 9. Having spoken thus to Hrishikesa (Lord of the senses), Arjuna (the conqueror of sleep), the destroyer of foes, said to Krishna: "I will not fight," and became silent. Tam uvaacha hrisheekeshah prahasanniva bhaarata; Senayor ubhayor madhye visheedantam idam vachah. 10. To him who was despondent in the midst of the two armies, Sri Krishna, as if smiling, O Bharata, spoke these words! Sri Bhagavaan Uvaacha: Ashochyaan anvashochastwam prajnaavaadaamshcha bhaashase; Gataasoon agataasoomshcha naanushochanti panditaah. The Blessed Lord said: 11. Thou hast grieved for those that should not be grieved for, yet thou speakest words of wisdom. The wise grieve neither for the living nor for the dead. Na twevaaham jaatu naasam na twam neme janaadhipaah; Na chaiva na bhavishyaamah sarve vayam atah param. 12. Nor at any time indeed was I not, nor these rulers of men, nor verily shall we ever cease to be hereafter. Dehino'smin yathaa dehe kaumaaram yauvanam jaraa; Tathaa dehaantara praaptir dheeras tatra na muhyati. 13. Just as in this body the embodied (soul) passes into childhood, youth and old age, so also does he pass into another body; the firm man does not grieve thereat. Maatraasparshaastu kaunteya sheetoshnasukhaduhkhadaah; Aagamaapaayino'nityaas taamstitikshaswa bhaarata. 19 BHAGAVAD GITA 14. The contacts of the senses with the objects, O son of Kunti, which cause heat and cold and pleasure and pain, have a beginning and an end; they are impermanent; endure them bravely, O Arjuna! Yam hi na vyathayantyete purusham purusharshabha; Samaduhkha sukham dheeram so'mritatwaaya kalpate. 15. That firm man whom surely these afflict not, O chief among men, to whom pleasure and pain are the same, is fit for attaining immortality! Naasato vidyate bhaavo naabhaavo vidyate satah; Ubhayorapi drishto'ntastwanayos tattwadarshibhih. 16. The unreal hath no being; there is no non-being of the Real; the truth about both has been seen by the knowers of the Truth (or the seers of the Essence). COMMENTARY: What is changing must always be unreal. What is constant or permanent must always be real. The Atman or the eternal, all-pervading Self ever exists. It is the only Reality. This phenomenal world of names and forms is ever changing. Names and forms are subject to decay and death. Hence they are unreal or impermanent. Avinaashi tu tad viddhi yena sarvam idam tatam; Vinaasham avyayasyaasya na kashchit kartum arhati. 17. Know That to be indestructible, by whom all this is pervaded. None can cause the destruction of That, the Imperishable. COMMENTARY: The Self pervades all objects like ether. Even if the pot is broken, the ether that is within and without it cannot be destroyed. Similarly, if the bodies and all other objects perish, the eternal Self that pervades them cannot be destroyed; It is the living Truth. Antavanta ime dehaa nityasyoktaah shareerinah; Anaashino'prameyasya tasmaad yudhyaswa bhaarata. 18. These bodies of the embodied Self, which is eternal, indestructible and immeasurable, are said to have an end. Therefore, fight, O Arjuna! Ya enam vetti hantaaram yashchainam manyate hatam; Ubhau tau na vijaaneeto naayam hanti na hanyate. 19. He who takes the Self to be the slayer and he who thinks He is slain, neither of them knows; He slays not nor is He slain. Na jaayate mriyate vaa kadaachin Naayam bhootwaa bhavitaa vaa na bhooyah; Ajo nityah shaashwato'yam puraano 20 SANKHYA YOGA Na hanyate hanyamaane shareere. 20. He is not born nor does He ever die; after having been, He again ceases not to be. Unborn, eternal, changeless and ancient, He is not killed when the body is killed, Vedaavinaashinam nityam ya enam ajam avyayam; Katham sa purushah paartha kam ghaatayati hanti kam. 21. Whosoever knows Him to be indestructible, eternal, unborn and inexhaustible, how can that man slay, O Arjuna, or cause to be slain? Vaasaamsi jeernaani yathaa vihaaya Navaani grihnaati naro'paraani; Tathaa shareeraani vihaaya jeernaa Nyanyaani samyaati navaani dehee. 22. Just as a man casts off worn-out clothes and puts on new ones, so also the embodied Self casts off worn-out bodies and enters others that are new. Nainam cchindanti shastraani nainam dahati paavakah; Na chainam kledayantyaapo na shoshayati maarutah. 23. Weapons cut It not, fire burns It not, water wets It not, wind dries It not. COMMENTARY: The Self is partless. It is infinite and extremely subtle. So the sword cannot cut It, fire cannot burn It, wind cannot dry It. Acchedyo'yam adaahyo'yam akledyo'shoshya eva cha; Nityah sarvagatah sthaanur achalo'yam sanaatanah. 24. This Self cannot be cut, burnt, wetted nor dried up. It is eternal, all-pervading, stable, ancient and immovable. Avyakto'yam achintyo'yam avikaaryo'yam uchyate; Tasmaad evam viditwainam naanushochitum arhasi. 25. This (Self) is said to be unmanifested, unthinkable and unchangeable. Therefore, knowing This to be such, thou shouldst not grieve. Atha chainam nityajaatam nityam vaa manyase mritam; Tathaapi twam mahaabaaho naivam shochitum arhasi. 26. But, even if thou thinkest of It as being constantly born and dying, even then, O mighty-armed, thou shouldst not grieve! 21 BHAGAVAD GITA COMMENTARY: Birth is inevitable to what is dead and death is inevitable to what is born. This is the law of Nature. Therefore, one should not grieve. Jaatasya hi dhruvo mrityur dhruvam janma mritasya cha; Tasmaad aparihaarye'rthe na twam shochitum arhasi. 27. For, certain is death for the born and certain is birth for the dead; therefore, over the inevitable thou shouldst not grieve. Avyaktaadeeni bhootaani vyaktamadhyaani bhaarata; Avyakta nidhanaanyeva tatra kaa paridevanaa. 28. Beings are unmanifested in their beginning, manifested in their middle state, O Arjuna, and unmanifested again in their end! What is there to grieve about? COMMENTARY: The physical body is a combination of the five elements. It is perceived by the physical eye only after the five elements have entered into such combination. After death the body disintegrates and all the five elements return to their source. The body cannot be perceived now. It can be perceived only in the middle state. He who understands the nature of the body and human relationships based upon it will not grieve. Aashcharyavat pashyati kashchid enam Aashcharyavad vadati tathaiva chaanyah; Aashcharyavacchainam anyah shrinoti Shrutwaapyenam veda na chaiva kashchit. 29. One sees This (the Self) as a wonder; another speaks of It as a wonder; another hears of It as a wonder; yet, having heard, none understands It at all. COMMENTARY: The verse may also be interpreted in this manner: he that sees, hears and speaks of the Self is a wonderful man. Such a man is very rare. He is one among many thousands. Therefore, the Self is very hard to understand. Dehee nityam avadhyo'yam dehe sarvasya bhaarata; Tasmaat sarvaani bhootaani na twam shochitum arhasi. 30. This, the Indweller in the body of everyone, is always indestructible, O Arjuna! Therefore, thou shouldst not grieve for any creature. Swadharmam api chaavekshya na vikampitum arhasi; Dharmyaaddhi yuddhaacchreyo'nyat kshatriyasya na vidyate. 31. Further, having regard to thy own duty, thou shouldst not waver, for there is nothing higher for a Kshatriya than a righteous war. 22 SANKHYA YOGA COMMENTARY: To a Kshatriya (one born in the warrior or ruling class) nothing is more welcome than a righteous war. Yadricchayaa chopapannam swargadwaaram apaavritam; Sukhinah kshatriyaah paartha labhante yuddham eedrisham. 32. Happy are the Kshatriyas, O Arjuna, who are called upon to fight in such a battle that comes of itself as an open door to heaven! COMMENTARY: The scriptures declare that if a warrior dies for a righteous cause on the battlefield he at once ascends to heaven. Atha chettwam imam dharmyam samgraamam na karishyasi; Tatah swadharmam keertim cha hitwaa paapam avaapsyasi. 33. But, if thou wilt not fight in this righteous war, then, having abandoned thine duty and fame, thou shalt incur sin. Akeertim chaapi bhootaani kathayishyanti te'vyayaam; Sambhaavitasya chaakeertir maranaad atirichyate. 34. People, too, will recount thy everlasting dishonour; and to one who has been honoured, dishonour is worse than death. Bhayaad ranaad uparatam mamsyante twaam mahaarathaah; Yeshaam cha twam bahumato bhootwaa yaasyasi laaghavam. 35. The great car-warriors will think that thou hast withdrawn from the battle through fear; and thou wilt be lightly held by them who have thought much of thee. Avaachyavaadaamshcha bahoon vadishyanti tavaahitaah; Nindantastava saamarthyam tato duhkhataram nu kim. 36. Thy enemies also, cavilling at thy power, will speak many abusive words. What is more painful than this! Hato vaa praapsyasi swargam jitwaa vaa bhokshyase maheem; Tasmaad uttishtha kaunteya yuddhaaya kritanishchayah. 37. Slain, thou wilt obtain heaven; victorious, thou wilt enjoy the earth; therefore, stand up, O son of Kunti, resolved to fight! Sukhaduhkhe same kritwaa laabhaalaabhau jayaajayau; Tato yuddhaaya yujyaswa naivam paapamavaapsyasi. 23 BHAGAVAD GITA 38. Having made pleasure and pain, gain and loss, victory and defeat the same, engage thou in battle for the sake of battle; thus thou shalt not incur sin. COMMENTARY: This is the Yoga of equanimity or the doctrine of poise in action. If a person performs actions with the above mental attitude, he will not reap the fruits of such actions. Eshaa te'bhihitaa saankhye buddhir yoge twimaam shrinu; Buddhyaa yukto yayaa paartha karma bandham prahaasyasi. 39. This which has been taught to thee, is wisdom concerning Sankhya. Now listen to wisdom concerning Yoga, endowed with which, O Arjuna, thou shalt cast off the bonds of action! Nehaabhikramanaasho'sti pratyavaayo na vidyate; Swalpam apyasya dharmasya traayate mahato bhayaat. 40. In this there is no loss of effort, nor is there any harm (the production of contrary results or transgression). Even a little of this knowledge (even a little practice of this Yoga) protects one from great fear. COMMENTARY: In Karma Yoga (selfless action) even a little effort brings immediate purification of the heart. Purification of the heart leads to fearlessness. Vyavasaayaatmikaa buddhir ekeha kurunandana; Bahushaakhaa hyanantaashcha buddhayo'vyavasaayinaam. 41. Here, O joy of the Kurus, there is a single one-pointed determination! Many-branched and endless are the thoughts of the irresolute. Yaam imaam pushpitaam vaacham pravadantyavipashchitah; Vedavaadarataah paartha naanyad asteeti vaadinah. 42. Flowery speech is uttered by the unwise, who take pleasure in the eulogising words of the Vedas, O Arjuna, saying: "There is nothing else!" COMMENTARY: Unwise people who lack discrimination place great stress upon the Karma Kanda or ritualistic portion of the Vedas which lays down specific rules for specific actions for the attainment of specific fruit. They extol these actions and rewards unduly. Kaamaatmaanah swargaparaa janmakarmaphalapradaam; Kriyaavisheshabahulaam bhogaishwaryagatim prati. 43. Full of desires, having heaven as their goal, they utter speech which promises birth as the reward of one's actions, and prescribe various specific actions for the attainment of pleasure and power. Bhogaishwarya prasaktaanaam tayaapahritachetasaam; 24 SANKHYA YOGA Vyavasaayaatmikaa buddhih samaadhau na vidheeyate. 44. For those who are much attached to pleasure and to power, whose minds are drawn away by such teaching, that determinate faculty is not manifest that is steadily bent on meditation and Samadhi (the state of Superconsciousness). Traigunyavishayaa vedaa nistraigunyo bhavaarjuna; Nirdwandwo nityasatwastho niryogakshema aatmavaan. 45. The Vedas deal with the three attributes (of Nature); be thou above these three attributes, O Arjuna! Free yourself from the pairs of opposites and ever remain in the quality of Sattwa (goodness), freed from the thought of acquisition and preservation, and be established in the Self. COMMENTARY: Guna means attribute or quality. It is substance as well as quality. Nature is made up of three Gunas—Sattwa (purity, light, harmony), Rajas (passion, restlessness, motion), and Tamas (inertia, darkness). The pairs of opposites are pleasure and pain, heat and cold, gain and loss, victory and defeat, honour and dishonour, praise and censure. Yaavaanartha udapaane sarvatah samplutodake; Taavaan sarveshu vedeshu braahmanasya vijaanatah. 46. To the Brahmana who has known the Self, all the Vedas are of as much use as is a reservoir of water in a place where there is a flood. COMMENTARY: Only for a sage who has realised the Self are the Vedas of no use, because he is in possession of knowledge of the Self. This does not, however, mean that the Vedas are useless. They are useful for neophytes or aspirants who have just started on the spiritual path. Karmanyevaadhikaaraste maa phaleshu kadaachana; Maa karmaphalahetur bhoor maa te sango'stwakarmani. 47. Thy right is to work only, but never with its fruits; let not the fruits of actions be thy motive, nor let thy attachment be to inaction. COMMENTARY: Actions done with expectation of its rewards bring bondage. If you do not thirst for them, you get purification of heart and ultimately knowledge of the Self. Yogasthah kuru karmaani sangam tyaktwaa dhananjaya; Siddhyasiddhyoh samo bhootwaa samatwam yoga uchyate. 48. Perform action, O Arjuna, being steadfast in Yoga, abandoning attachment and balanced in success and failure! Evenness of mind is called Yoga. Doorena hyavaram karma buddhiyogaad dhananjaya; Buddhau sharanamanwiccha kripanaah phalahetavah. 25 BHAGAVAD GITA 49. Far lower than the Yoga of wisdom is action, O Arjuna! Seek thou refuge in wisdom; wretched are they whose motive is the fruit. COMMENTARY: Actions done with evenness of mind is the Yoga of wisdom. Actions performed by one who expects their fruits are far inferior to the Yoga of wisdom wherein the seeker does not seek the fruits. The former leads to bondage, and is the cause of birth and death. Buddhiyukto jahaateeha ubhe sukrita dushkrite; Tasmaad yogaaya yujyaswa yogah karmasu kaushalam. 50. Endowed with wisdom (evenness of mind), one casts off in this life both good and evil deeds; therefore, devote thyself to Yoga; Yoga is skill in action. COMMENTARY: Actions which are of a binding nature lose that nature when performed with equanimity of mind. Karmajam buddhiyuktaa hi phalam tyaktwaa maneeshinah; Janmabandha vinirmuktaah padam gacchantyanaamayam. 51. The wise, possessed of knowledge, having abandoned the fruits of their actions, and being freed from the fetters of birth, go to the place which is beyond all evil. COMMENTARY: Clinging to the fruits of actions is the cause of rebirth. Man has to take a body to enjoy them. If actions are done for the sake of God, without desire for the fruits, one is released from the bonds of birth and death and attains to immortal bliss. Yadaa te mohakalilam buddhir vyatitarishyati; Tadaa gantaasi nirvedam shrotavyasya shrutasya cha. 52. When thy intellect crosses beyond the mire of delusion, then thou shalt attain to indifference as to what has been heard and what has yet to be heard. COMMENTARY: The mire of delusion is identification of the Self with the body and mind. Shrutivipratipannaa te yadaa sthaasyati nishchalaa; Samaadhaavachalaa buddhistadaa yogam avaapsyasi. 53. When thy intellect, perplexed by what thou hast heard, shall stand immovable and steady in the Self, then thou shalt attain Self-realisation. Arjuna Uvaacha: Sthitaprajnasya kaa bhaashaa samaadhisthasya keshava; Sthitadheeh kim prabhaasheta kimaaseeta vrajeta kim. Arjuna said: 26 SANKHYA YOGA 54. What, O Krishna, is the description of him who has steady wisdom and is merged in the Superconscious State? How does one of steady wisdom speak? How does he sit? How does he walk? Sri Bhagavaan Uvaacha: Prajahaati yadaa kaamaan sarvaan paartha manogataan; Aatmanyevaatmanaa tushtah sthitaprajnastadochyate. The Blessed Lord said: 55. When a man completely casts off, O Arjuna, all the desires of the mind and is satisfied in the Self by the Self, then is he said to be one of steady wisdom! COMMENTARY: All the pleasures of the world are worthless to an illumined sage who is ever content in the immortal Self. Duhkheshwanudwignamanaah sukheshu vigatasprihah; Veetaraagabhayakrodhah sthitadheer munir uchyate. 56. He whose mind is not shaken by adversity, who does not hanker after pleasures, and who is free from attachment, fear and anger, is called a sage of steady wisdom. Yah sarvatraanabhisnehas tattat praapya shubhaashubham; Naabhinandati na dweshti tasya prajnaa pratishthitaa. 57. He who is everywhere without attachment, on meeting with anything good or bad, who neither rejoices nor hates, his wisdom is fixed. Yadaa samharate chaayam kurmo'ngaaneeva sarvashah; Indriyaaneendriyaarthebhyas tasya prajnaa pratishthitaa. 58. When, like the tortoise which withdraws its limbs on all sides, he withdraws his senses from the sense-objects, then his wisdom becomes steady. Vishayaa vinivartante niraahaarasya dehinah Rasavarjam raso'pyasya param drishtwaa nivartate. 59. The objects of the senses turn away from the abstinent man, leaving the longing (behind); but his longing also turns away on seeing the Supreme. Yatato hyapi kaunteya purushasya vipashchitah; Indriyaani pramaatheeni haranti prasabham manah. 60. The turbulent senses, O Arjuna, do violently carry away the mind of a wise man though he be striving (to control them)! 27 BHAGAVAD GITA Taani sarvaani samyamya yukta aaseeta matparah; Vashe hi yasyendriyaani tasya prajnaa pratishthitaa. 61. Having restrained them all he should sit steadfast, intent on Me; his wisdom is steady whose senses are under control. Dhyaayato vishayaan pumsah sangas teshupajaayate; Sangaat sanjaayate kaamah kaamaat krodho'bhijaayate. 62. When a man thinks of the objects, attachment to them arises; from attachment desire is born; from desire anger arises. Krodhaad bhavati sammohah sammohaat smriti vibhramah; Smritibhramshaad buddhinaasho buddhinaashaat pranashyati. 63. From anger comes delusion; from delusion the loss of memory; from loss of memory the destruction of discrimination; from the destruction of discrimination he perishes. Raagadwesha viyuktaistu vishayaanindriyaishcharan; Aatmavashyair vidheyaatmaa prasaadamadhigacchati. 64. But the self-controlled man, moving amongst objects with the senses under restraint, and free from attraction and repulsion, attains to peace. Prasaade sarvaduhkhaanaam haanir asyopajaayate; Prasannachetaso hyaashu buddhih paryavatishthate. 65. In that peace all pains are destroyed, for the intellect of the tranquil-minded soon becomes steady. COMMENTARY: When peace is attained all miseries end. Naasti buddhir ayuktasya na chaayuktasya bhaavanaa; Na chaabhaavayatah shaantir ashaantasya kutah sukham. 66. There is no knowledge of the Self to the unsteady, and to the unsteady no meditation is possible; and to the un-meditative there can be no peace; and to the man who has no peace, how can there be happiness? Indriyaanaam hi charataam yanmano'nuvidheeyate; Tadasya harati prajnaam vaayur naavam ivaambhasi. 67. For the mind which follows in the wake of the wandering senses, carries away his discrimination as the wind (carries away) a boat on the waters. Tasmaad yasya mahaabaaho nigriheetaani sarvashah; 28 SANKHYA YOGA Indriyaaneendriyaarthebhyas tasya prajnaa pratishthitaa. 68. Therefore, O mighty-armed Arjuna, his knowledge is steady whose senses are completely restrained from sense-objects! Yaanishaa sarvabhootaanaam tasyaam jaagarti samyamee; Yasyaam jaagrati bhootaani saa nishaa pashyato muneh. 69. That which is night to all beings, then the self-controlled man is awake; when all beings are awake, that is night for the sage who sees. COMMENTARY: The sage lives in the Self; this is day to him. He is unconscious of worldly phenomena; this is like night to him. The ordinary man is unconscious of his real nature. So life in the Self is like night to him. He experiences sense-objects; this is day to him. Aapooryamaanam achalapratishtham Samudram aapah pravishanti yadwat; Tadwat kaamaa yam pravishanti sarve Sa shaantim aapnoti na kaamakaami. 70. He attains peace into whom all desires enter as waters enter the ocean, which, filled from all sides, remains unmoved; but not the man who is full of desires. Vihaaya kaamaan yah sarvaan pumaamshcharati nihsprihah; Nirmamo nirahankaarah sa shaantim adhigacchati. 71. The man attains peace, who, abandoning all desires, moves about without longing, without the sense of mine and without egoism. Eshaa braahmee sthitih paartha nainaam praapya vimuhyati; Sthitwaasyaamantakaale'pi brahmanirvaanamricchati. 72. This is the Brahmic seat (eternal state), O son of Pritha! Attaining to this, none is deluded. Being established therein, even at the end of life one attains to oneness with Brahman. Hari Om Tat Sat Iti Srimad Bhagavadgeetaasoopanishatsu Brahmavidyaayaam Yogashaastre Sri Krishnaarjunasamvaade Saankhyayogo Naama Dvitiyo'dhyaayah Thus in the Upanishads of the glorious Bhagavad Gita, the science of the Eternal, the scripture of Yoga, the dialogue between Sri Krishna and Arjuna, ends the second discourse entitled: "The Sankhya Yoga"

CHAPTER SEVEN

Summary of Third Discourse

In order to remove Moha or attachment, which was the sole cause of Arjuna's delusion, Sri Krishna taught him the imperishable nature of the Atman, the realisation of which would grant him the freedom of the Eternal. A doubt therefore arises in Arjuna's mind as to the necessity of engaging in action even after one has attained this state. Sri Krishna clears this doubt by telling him that although one has realised oneness with the Eternal, one has to perform action through the force of Prakriti or Nature. He emphasises that perfection is attained not by ceasing to engage in action but by doing all actions as a divine offering, imbued with a spirit of non-attachment and sacrifice. The man of God-vision, Sri Krishna explains to Arjuna, need not engage in action, as he has attained everything that has to be attained. He can be ever absorbed in the calm and immutable Self. But to perform action for the good of the world and for the education of the masses is no doubt superior. Therefore, action is necessary not only for one who has attained perfection but also for one who is striving for perfection. Sri Krishna quotes the example of Janaka, the great sage-king of India, who continued to rule his kingdom even after attaining God-realisation. Prakriti or Nature is made up of the three qualities—Rajas, Tamas and Sattwa. The Atman is beyond these three qualities and their functions. Only when knowledge of this fact dawns in man does he attain perfection. The Lord tells Arjuna that each one should do his duty according to his nature, and that doing duty that is suited to one's nature in the right spirit of detachment will lead to perfection. Arjuna raises the question as to why man commits such actions that cloud his mind and drag him downwards, by force, as it were. Sri Krishna answers that it is desire that impels man to lose his discrimination and understanding, and thus commit wrong actions. Desire is the root cause of all evil actions. If desire is removed, then the divine power manifests in its full glory and one enjoys peace, bliss, light and freedom. Arjuna Uvaacha Jyaayasee chet karmanaste mataa buddhir janaardana; Tat kim karmani ghore maam niyojayasi keshava. Arjuna said: 1. If it be thought by Thee that knowledge is superior to action, O Krishna, why then, O Kesava, dost Thou ask me to engage in this terrible action? 30 THE YOGA OF ACTION Vyaamishreneva vaakyena buddhim mohayaseeva me; Tadekam vada nishchitya yena shreyo'ham aapnuyaam. 2. With these apparently perplexing words Thou confusest, as it were, my understanding; therefore, tell me that one way for certain by which I may attain bliss. Sri Bhagavaan Uvaacha: Loke'smin dwividhaa nishthaa puraa proktaa mayaanagha; Jnaanayogena saankhyaanaam karmayogena yoginaam. The Blessed Lord said: 3. In this world there is a twofold path, as I said before, O sinless one,—the path of knowledge of the Sankhyas and the path of action of the Yogis! Na karmanaam anaarambhaan naishkarmyam purusho'shnute; Na cha sannyasanaad eva siddhim samadhigacchati. 4. Not by the non-performance of actions does man reach actionlessness, nor by mere renunciation does he attain to perfection. COMMENTARY: Even if a man abandons action, his mind may be active. One cannot reach perfection or freedom from action or knowledge of the Self, merely by renouncing action. He must possess knowledge of the Self. Na hi kashchit kshanamapi jaatu tishthatyakarmakrit; Kaaryate hyavashah karma sarvah prakritijair gunaih. 5. Verily none can ever remain for even a moment without performing action; for, everyone is made to act helplessly indeed by the qualities born of Nature. COMMENTARY: The ignorant man is driven to action helplessly by the actions of the Gunas—Rajas, Tamas and Sattwa. Karmendriyaani samyamya ya aaste manasaa smaran; Indriyaarthaan vimoodhaatmaa mithyaachaarah sa uchyate. 6. He who, restraining the organs of action, sits thinking of the sense-objects in mind, he, of deluded understanding, is called a hypocrite. Yastwindriyaani manasaa niyamyaarabhate'rjuna; Karmendriyaih karmayogam asaktah sa vishishyate. 7. But whosoever, controlling the senses by the mind, O Arjuna, engages himself in Karma Yoga with the organs of action, without attachment, he excels! 31 BHAGAVAD GITA Niyatam kuru karma twam karma jyaayo hyakarmanah; Shareerayaatraapi cha te na prasiddhyed akarmanah. 8. Do thou perform thy bounden duty, for action is superior to inaction and even the maintenance of the body would not be possible for thee by inaction. Yajnaarthaat karmano'nyatra loko'yam karmabandhanah; Tadartham karma kaunteya muktasangah samaachara. 9. The world is bound by actions other than those performed for the sake of sacrifice; do thou, therefore, O son of Kunti,

perform action for that sake (for sacrifice) alone, free from attachment!
COMMENTARY: If anyone does actions for the sake of the Lord, he is not
bound. His heart is purified by performing actions for the sake of the Lord.
Where this spirit of unselfishness does not govern the action, such actions
bind one to worldliness, however good or glorious they may be. Sahayajnaah
prajaah srishtwaa purovaacha prajaapatih; Anena prasavishyadhwam esha
vo'stvishtakaamadhuk. 10. The Creator, having in the beginning of creation
created mankind together with sacrifice, said: "By this shall ye propagate;
let this be the milch cow of your desires (the cow which yields the desired
objects)". Devaan bhaavayataanena te devaa bhaavayantu vah; Parasparam
bhaavayantah shreyah param avaapsyatha. 11. With this do ye nourish the
gods, and may the gods nourish you; thus nourishing one another, ye shall
attain to the highest good. Ishtaan bhogaan hi vo devaa daasyante
yajnabhaavitaah; Tair dattaan apradaayaibhyo yo bhungkte stena eva sah.
12. The gods, nourished by the sacrifice, will give you the desired objects.
So, he who enjoys the objects given by the gods without offering (in return)
to them, is verily a thief. Yajnashishtaashinah santo muchyante sarva
kilbishaih; Bhunjate te twagham paapaa ye pachantyaatma kaaranaat. 13.
The righteous, who eat of the remnants of the sacrifice, are freed from all
sins; but those sinful ones who cook food (only) for their own sake, verily
eat sin. Annaad bhavanti bhootaani parjanyaad anna sambhavah; Yajnaad
bhavati parjanyo yajnah karma samudbhavah. 32 THE YOGA OF ACTION
14. From food come forth beings, and from rain food is produced; from
sacrifice arises rain, and sacrifice is born of action. Karma brahmodbhavam
viddhi brahmaakshara samudbhavam; Tasmaat sarvagatam brahma nityam
yajne pratishthitam. 15. Know thou that action comes from Brahma, and
Brahma proceeds from the Imperishable. Therefore, the all-pervading
(Brahma) ever rests in sacrifice. Evam pravartitam chakram
naanuvartayateeha yah; Aghaayur indriyaaraamo mogham paartha sa
jeevati. 16. He who does not follow the wheel thus set revolving, who
is of sinful life, rejoicing in the senses, he lives in vain, O Arjuna!
COMMENTARY: He who does not follow the wheel by studying the Vedas
and performing the sacrifices prescribed therein, but who indulges only
in sensual pleasures, lives in vain. He wastes his life. Yastwaatmaratir eva
syaad aatmatriptashcha maanavah; Aatmanyeva cha santushtas tasya
kaaryam na vidyate. 17. But for that man who rejoices only in the Self,
who is satisfied in the Self, who is content in the Self alone, verily there is
nothing to do. Naiva tasya kritenaartho naakriteneha kashchana; Na chaasya

sarvabhooteshu kashchidartha vyapaashrayah. 18. For him there is no interest whatsoever in what is done or what is not done; nor does he depend on any being for any object. COMMENTARY: The sage who rejoices in his own Self does not gain anything by doing any action. To him no real purpose is served by engaging in any action. No evil can touch him as a result of inaction. He does not lose anything by being inactive. Tasmaad asaktah satatam kaaryam karma samaachara; Asakto hyaacharan karma param aapnoti poorushah. 19. Therefore, without attachment, do thou always perform action which should be done; for, by performing action without attachment man reaches the Supreme. Karmanaiva hi samsiddhim aasthitaa janakaadayah; Lokasangraham evaapi sampashyan kartum arhasi. 20. Janaka and others attained perfection verily by action only; even with a view to the protection of the masses thou shouldst perform action. 33 BHAGAVAD GITA Yadyad aacharati shreshthas tattadevetaro janah; Sa yat pramaanam kurute lokas tad anuvartate. 21. Whatsoever a great man does, that other men also do; whatever he sets up as the standard, that the world follows. Na me paarthaasti kartavyam trishu lokeshu kinchana; Naanavaaptam avaaptavyam varta eva cha karmani. 22. There is nothing in the three worlds, O Arjuna, that should be done by Me, nor is there anything unattained that should be attained; yet I engage Myself in action! Yadi hyaham na varteyam jaatu karmanyatandritah; Mama vartmaanuvartante manushyaah paartha sarvashah. 23. For, should I not ever engage Myself in action, unwearied, men would in every way follow My path, O Arjuna! Utseedeyur ime lokaa na kuryaam karma ched aham; Sankarasya cha kartaa syaam upahanyaam imaah prajaah. 24. These worlds would perish if I did not perform action; I should be the author of confusion of castes and destruction of these beings. Saktaah karmanyavidwaamso yathaa kurvanti bhaarata; Kuryaad vidwaam stathaa saktash chikeershur lokasangraham. 25. As the ignorant men act from attachment to action, O Bharata (Arjuna), so should the wise act without attachment, wishing the welfare of the world! Na buddhibhedam janayed ajnaanaam karmasanginaam; Joshayet sarva karmaani vidwaan yuktah samaacharan. 26. Let no wise man unsettle the minds of ignorant people who are attached to action; he should engage them in all actions, himself fulfilling them with devotion. Prakriteh kriyamaanaani gunaih karmaani sarvashah; Ahamkaaravimoodhaatmaa kartaaham iti manyate. 27. All actions are wrought in all cases by the qualities of Nature only. He whose mind is deluded by egoism thinks: "I am the doer". COMMENTARY: Prakriti or Nature is that state in which the three Gunas exist in a state of equilibrium. When this equilibrium is disturbed, creation begins and the body, senses and mind are formed. The man who is deluded by egoism identifies the Self with the body, mind, the 34 THE YOGA OF ACTION life-force and the senses, and ascribes to the Self all the attributes of the body and the senses. In reality the Gunas of nature perform all actions. Tattwavittu mahaabaaho gunakarma vibhaagayoh; Gunaa guneshu vartanta iti matwaa na sajjate. 28. But he who knows the truth, O mighty-armed Arjuna, about the divisions of the qualities and their functions, knowing that the Gunas as senses move amidst the Gunas as the sense-objects, is not attached. Prakriter gunasammoodhaah sajjante gunakarmasu; Taan akritsnavido mandaan kritsnavin na vichaalayet. 29. Those deluded by the qualities of Nature are attached to the functions of the qualities. A man of perfect knowledge should not unsettle the foolish one of imperfect knowledge. Mayi sarvaani karmaani sannyasyaadhyaatma chetasaa; Niraasheer nirmamo bhootwaa yudhyaswa vigatajwarah. 30. Renouncing all actions in Me, with the mind centred in the Self, free from hope and egoism, and from (mental) fever, do thou fight. COMMENTARY: Surrender all actions to Me with the thought: "I perform all actions for the sake of the Lord only." Ye me matam idam nityam anutishthanti maanavaah; Shraddhaavanto'nasooyanto muchyante te'pi karmabhih. 31. Those men who constantly practise this teaching of Mine with faith and without cavilling, they too are freed from actions. Ye twetad abhyasooyanto naanutishthanti me matam; Sarvajnaanavimoodhaam staan viddhi nashtaan achetasah. 32. But those who carp at My teaching and do not practise it, deluded in all knowledge and devoid of discrimination, know them to be doomed to destruction. Sadrisham cheshtate swasyaah prakriter jnaanavaan api; Prakritim yaanti bhootaani nigrahah kim karishyati. 33. Even a wise man acts in accordance with his own nature; beings will follow nature; what can restraint do? COMMENTARY: Only the ignorant man comes under the sway of his natural propensities. The seeker after Truth who is endowed with the 'Four Means' and who constantly 35 BHAGAVAD GITA practises meditation, can easily control Nature if he rises above the sway of the pairs of opposites, like love and hate, etc. Indriyasyendriyasyaarthe raagadweshau vyavasthitau; Tayor na vasham aagacchet tau hyasya paripanthinau. 34. Attachment and aversion for the objects of the senses abide in the senses; let none come under their sway, for they are his foes. Shreyaan swadharmo vigunah paradharmaat swanushthitaat; Swadharme nidhanam shreyah paradharmo bhayaavahah.

35. Better is one's own duty, though devoid of merit, than the duty of another well discharged. Better is death in one's own duty; the duty of another is fraught with fear. Arjuna Uvaacha: Atha kena prayukto'yam paapam charati poorushah; Anicchann api vaarshneya balaad iva niyojitah. Arjuna said: 36. But impelled by what does man commit sin, though against his wishes, O Varshneya (Krishna), constrained, as it were, by force? Sri Bhagavaan Uvaacha: Kaama esha krodha esha rajoguna samudbhavah; Mahaashano mahaapaapmaa viddhyenam iha vairinam. The Blessed Lord said: 37. It is desire, it is anger born of the quality of Rajas, all-sinful and all-devouring; know this as the foe here (in this world). Dhoomenaavriyate vahnir yathaadarsho malena cha; Yatholbenaavrito garbhas tathaa tenedam aavritam. 38. As fire is enveloped by smoke, as a mirror by dust, and as an embryo by the amnion, so is this enveloped by that. Aavritam jnaanam etena jnaanino nityavairinaa; Kaamaroopena kaunteya dushpoorenaanalena cha. 39. O Arjuna, wisdom is enveloped by this constant enemy of the wise in the form of desire, which is unappeasable as fire! Indriyaani mano buddhir asyaadhishthaanam uchyate; 36 THE YOGA OF ACTION Etair vimohayatyesha jnaanam aavritya dehinam. 40. The senses, mind and intellect are said to be its seat; through these it deludes the embodied by veiling his wisdom. Tasmaat twam indriyaanyaadau niyamya bharatarshabha; Paapmaanam prajahi hyenam jnaana vijnaana naashanam. 41. Therefore, O best of the Bharatas (Arjuna), controlling the senses first, do thou kill this sinful thing (desire), the destroyer of knowledge and realisation! Indriyaani paraanyaahur indriyebhyah param manah; Manasastu paraa buddhir yo buddheh paratastu sah. 42. They say that the senses are superior (to the body); superior to the senses is the mind; superior to the mind is the intellect; and one who is superior even to the intellect is He—the Self. Evam buddheh param buddhwaa samstabhyaatmaanam aatmanaa; Jahi shatrum mahaabaaho kaamaroopam duraasadam. 43. Thus, knowing Him who is superior to the intellect and restraining the self by the Self, slay thou, O mighty-armed Arjuna, the enemy in the form of desire, hard to conquer! COMMENTARY: Restrain the lower self by the higher Self. Subdue the lower mind by the higher mind. It is difficult to conquer desire because it is of a highly complex and incomprehensible nature. But a man of discrimination and dispassion, who does constant and intense Sadhana, can conquer it quite easily.

CHAPTER EIGHT

Summary of Fourth Discourse

Lord Krishna declares that He is born from age to age, in order to raise man and take him to the Supreme. Whenever there is a prevalence of unrighteousness and the world is ruled by the forces of darkness, the Lord manifests Himself to destroy these adverse forces and to establish peace, order and harmony. Hence we see the appearance of the great saviours of the world. What is the secret of Yogic action? This the Lord proceeds to explain to Arjuna. Even though one is not engaged in action, but if the mind is active with the idea of doership and egoism, then it is action in inaction. On the other hand, though engaged physically in intense action, if the idea of agency is absent, if one feels that Prakriti does everything, it is inaction in action. The liberated man is free from attachment and is always calm and serene though engaged in ceaseless action. He is unaffected by the pairs of opposites like joy and grief, success and failure. One who has true union with the Lord is not subject to rebirth. He attains immortality. Such a union can only be achieved when one is free from attachment, fear and anger, being thoroughly purified by right knowledge. The Lord accepts the devotion of all, whatever path they may use to approach Him. Various kinds of sacrifices are performed by those engaged in the path to God. Through the practice of these sacrifices the mind is purified and led Godward. Here also there must be the spirit of non-attachment to the fruits of actions. Divine wisdom, according to Sri Krishna, should be sought at the feet of a liberated Guru, one who has realised the Truth. The aspirant should approach such a sage in a spirit of humility and devotion. God Himself manifests in the heart of the Guru and instructs the disciple. Having understood the Truth from the Guru by direct intuitive experience the aspirant is no longer deluded by ignorance. The liberated aspirant directly beholds the Self in all beings and all beings in the Self. He cognises through internal experience or intuition that all beings, from the Creator down to a blade of grass, exist in his own Self and also in God. Arjuna is given the most heartening assurance that divine wisdom liberates even the most sinful. When knowledge of the Self dawns, all actions with their results are burnt by the fire of that knowledge, just as fuel is burnt by fire. When there is no idea of egoism, when there is no desire for the fruits of one's actions, actions are no actions. They lose their potency. In order to attain divine wisdom one must have supreme faith and devotion. Faith is therefore the most important qualification for a spiritual aspirant. The doubting mind is always led 38 THE YOGA OF WISDOM astray from the right path. Faith ultimately confers divine knowledge, which removes ignorance once and for all. Mere intellectual knowledge does not lead to liberation. It cannot grant one supreme peace and freedom. When one has achieved complete self-mastery and self-control, when one has intense faith and devotion, then true knowledge dawns within and one attains liberation and freedom from all weaknesses and sins. The Lord concludes by emphasising that the soul that doubts goes to destruction. Without faith in oneself, in the scriptures and in the words of the preceptor, one cannot make any headway on the spiritual path. It is doubt that prevents one from engaging in spiritual Sadhana and realising the highest knowledge and bliss. By following the instructions of the Guru and through sincere service, one's doubts are rent asunder and divine knowledge manifests itself within. Spiritual progress then goes on at a rapid pace. Sri Bhagavaan Uvaacha: Imam vivaswate yogam proktavaan aham avyayam; Vivaswaan manave praaha manur ikshwaakave'braveet. The Blessed Lord said: 1. I taught this imperishable Yoga to Vivasvan; he told it to Manu; Manu proclaimed it to Ikshvaku. Evam paramparaa praaptam imam raajarshayo viduh; Sa kaaleneha mahataa yogo nashtah parantapa. 2. This, handed down thus in regular succession, the royal sages knew. This Yoga, by a long lapse of time, has been lost here, O Parantapa (burner of foes)! COMMENTARY: The royal sages were kings who at the same time possessed divine knowledge. They learnt this Yoga. Sa evaayam mayaa te'dya yogah proktah puraatanah; Bhakto'si me sakhaa cheti rahasyam hyetad uttamam. 3. That same ancient Yoga has been today taught to thee by Me, for, thou art My devotee and friend; it is the supreme secret. COMMENTARY: This ancient Yoga consists of profound and subtle teachings. Hence it is the supreme secret which the Lord reveals to Arjuna. Arjuna Uvaacha: Aparam bhavato janma param janma vivaswatah; 39 BHAGAVAD GITA Katham etadvijaaneeyaam twam aadau proktavaan iti. Arjuna said: 4. Later on was Thy birth, and prior to it was the birth of Vivasvan (the Sun); how am I to understand that Thou didst teach this Yoga in the beginning? Sri Bhagavaan Uvaacha: Bahooni me vyateetaani janmaani tava chaarjuna; Taanyaham veda sarvaani na twam vettha parantapa. The Blessed Lord said: 5. Many births of Mine have passed, as well as of thine, O Arjuna! I know them all but thou knowest not, O Parantapa! Ajo'pi sannavyayaatmaa bhootaanaam eeshwaro'pi san; Prakritim swaam adhishthaaya sambhavaamyaatmamaayayaa. 6. Though I am unborn and of imperishable nature, and though I am the Lord of all beings, yet, ruling over My own Nature, I am born by My own Maya. Yadaa yadaa hi dharmasya glaanir bhavati bhaarata; Abhyutthaanam adharmasya tadaatmaanam srijaamyaham. 7. Whenever there is a decline of righteousness, O Arjuna, and rise of unrighteousness, then I manifest Myself! COMMENTARY: That which elevates a man and helps him to reach the goal of life and attain knowledge is Dharma (righteousness); that which drags him into worldliness is unrighteousness. That which helps a man to attain liberation is Dharma; that which makes him irreligious is Adharma or unrighteousness. Paritraanaaya saadhoonaam vinaashaaya cha dushkritaam; Dharma samsthaapanaarthaaya sambhavaami yuge yuge. 8. For the protection of the good, for the destruction of the wicked, and for the establishment of righteousness, I am born in every age. Janma karma cha me divyam evam yo vetti tattwatah; Tyaktwa deham punarjanma naiti maameti so'rjuna. 9. He who thus knows in true light My divine birth and action, after having abandoned the body is not born again; he comes to Me, O Arjuna! Veetaraagabhayakrodhaa manmayaa maam upaashritaah; Bahavo jnaana tapasaa pootaa madbhaavam aagataah. 40 THE YOGA OF WISDOM 10. Freed from attachment, fear and anger, absorbed in Me, taking refuge in Me, purified by the fire of knowledge, many have attained to My Being. Ye yathaa maam prapadyante taamstathaiva bhajaamyaham; Mama vartmaanuvartante manushyaah paartha sarvashah. 11. In whatever way men approach Me, even so do I reward them; My path do men tread in all ways, O Arjuna! Kaangkshantah karmanaam siddhim yajanta iha devataah; Kshipram hi maanushe loke siddhir bhavati karmajaa. 12. Those who long for success in action in this world sacrifice to the gods, because success is quickly attained by men through action. Chaaturvarnyam mayaa srishtam gunakarma vibhaagashah; Tasya kartaaram api maam viddhyakartaaram avyayam. 13. The fourfold caste has been created by Me according to the differentiation of Guna and Karma; though I am the author thereof, know Me as the non-doer and immutable. COMMENTARY: The four castes are Brahmana, Kshatriya, Vaisya and Sudra. This division is according to the Guna and Karma. Guna is quality. Karma is the kind of work. Both Guna and Karma determine the caste of a man. In a Brahmana, Sattwa predominates. He possesses serenity, purity, self-restraint, straightforwardness and devotion. In a Kshatriya, Rajas predominates. He possesses prowess, splendour, firmness, dexterity, generosity and rulership. In a Vaisya, Rajas predominates and Tamas is subordinate to Rajas. He does the duty of ploughing, protection of cattle and trade. In a Sudra, Tamas predominates and Rajas is subordinate to the quality of Tamas. He renders service to the other three castes. Human temperaments and tendencies vary according to the Gunas. Na maam karmaani limpanti na me karmaphale sprihaa; Iti maam yo'bhijaanaati karmabhir na sa badhyate. 14. Actions do not taint Me, nor have I a desire for the fruits of actions. He who knows Me thus is not bound by actions. Evam jnaatwaa kritam karma poorvair api mumukshubhih; Kuru karmaiva tasmaat twam poorvaih poorvataram kritam. 41 BHAGAVAD GITA 15. Having known this, the ancient seekers after freedom also performed actions; therefore, do thou perform actions as did the ancients in days of yore. Kim karma kim akarmeti kavayo'pyatra mohitaah; Tat te karma pravakshyaami yajjnaatwaa mokshyase'shubhaat. 16. What is action? What is inaction? As to this even the wise are confused. Therefore, I shall teach thee such action (the nature of action and inaction), by knowing which thou shalt be liberated from the evil (of Samsara, the world of birth and death). Karmano hyapi boddhavyam boddhavyam cha vikarmanah; Akarmanashcha boddhavyam gahanaa karmano gatih. 17. For, verily the true nature of action (enjoined by the scriptures) should be known, also (that) of forbidden (or unlawful) action, and of inaction; hard to understand is the nature (path) of action. Karmanyakarma yah pashyed akarmani cha karma yah; Sa buddhimaan manushyeshu sa yuktah kritsnakarmakrit. 18. He who seeth inaction in action and action in inaction, he is wise among men; he is a Yogi and performer of all actions. COMMENTARY: It is the idea of agency, the idea of "I am the doer" that binds man to worldliness. If this idea vanishes, action is no action at all. It does not bind one to worldliness. This is inaction in action. But if a man sits quietly, thinking of actions and that he is their doer, he is ever doing actions. This is referred to as action in inaction. Yasya sarve samaarambhaah kaamasankalpa varjitaah;

Jnaanaagni dagdhakarmaanam tam aahuh panditam budhaah. 19. He whose undertakings are all devoid of desires and (selfish) purposes, and whose actions have been burnt by the fire of knowledge,—him the wise call a sage. Tyaktwaa karmaphalaasangam nityatripto niraashrayah; Karmanyabhipravritto'pi naiva kinchit karoti sah. 20. Having abandoned attachment to the fruit of the action, ever content, depending on nothing, he does not do anything though engaged in activity. Niraasheer yatachittaatmaa tyaktasarvaparigrahah; Shaareeram kevalam karma kurvannaapnoti kilbisham. 21. Without hope and with the mind and the self controlled, having abandoned all greed, doing mere bodily action, he incurs no sin. 42 THE YOGA OF WISDOM Yadricchaalaabhasantushto dwandwaateeto vimatsarah; Samah siddhaavasiddhau cha kritwaapi na nibadhyate. 22. Content with what comes to him without effort, free from the pairs of opposites and envy, even-minded in success and failure, though acting, he is not bound. Gatasangasya muktasya jnaanaavasthitachetasah; Yajnaayaacharatah karma samagram pravileeyate. 23. To one who is devoid of attachment, who is liberated, whose mind is established in knowledge, who works for the sake of sacrifice (for the sake of God), the whole action is dissolved. Brahmaarpanam brahmahavirbrahmaagnau brahmanaa hutam; Brahmaiva tena gantavyam brahmakarmasamaadhinaa. 24. Brahman is the oblation; Brahman is the melted butter (ghee); by Brahman is the oblation poured into the fire of Brahman; Brahman verily shall be reached by him who always sees Brahman in action. COMMENTARY: This is wisdom-sacrifice, wherein the idea of Brahman is substituted for the ideas of the instrument and other accessories of action, the idea of action itself and its results. By having such an idea the whole action melts away. Daivam evaapare yajnam yoginah paryupaasate; Brahmaagnaavapare yajnam yajnenaivopajuhwati. 25. Some Yogis perform sacrifice to the gods alone, while others (who have realised the Self) offer the Self as sacrifice by the Self in the fire of Brahman alone. Shrotraadeeneendriyaanyanye samyamaagnishu juhwati; Shabdaadeen vishayaananya indriyaagnishu juhwati. 26. Some again offer hearing and other senses as sacrifice in the fire of restraint; others offer sound and various objects of the senses as sacrifice in the fire of the senses. Sarvaaneendriya karmaani praanakarmaani chaapare; Aatmasamyamayogaagnau juhwati jnaanadeepite. 27. Others again sacrifice all the functions of the senses and those of the breath (vital energy or Prana) in the fire of the Yoga of self-restraint kindled by knowledge. Dravyayajnaas tapoyajnaa yogayajnaastathaapare;

Swaadhyaayajnaana yajnaashcha yatayah samshitavrataah. 28. Some again offer wealth, austerity and Yoga as sacrifice, while the ascetics of self-restraint and rigid vows offer study of scriptures and knowledge as sacrifice. 43 BHAGAVAD GITA Apaane juhwati praanam praane'paanam tathaa'pare; Praanaapaana gatee ruddhwaa praanaayaamaparaayanaah. 29. Others offer as sacrifice the outgoing breath in the incoming, and the incoming in the outgoing, restraining the courses of the outgoing and the incoming breaths, solely absorbed in the restraint of the breath. COMMENTARY: Some Yogis practise inhalation, some practise exhalation, and some retention of breath. This is Pranayama. Apare niyataahaaraah praanaan praaneshu juhwati; Sarve'pyete yajnavido yajnakshapita kalmashaah. 30. Others who regulate their diet offer life-breaths in life-breaths; all these are knowers of sacrifice, whose sins are all destroyed by sacrifice. Yajnashishtaamritabhujo yaanti brahma sanaatanam; Naayam loko'styayajnasya kuto'nyah kurusattama. 31. Those who eat the remnants of the sacrifice, which are like nectar, go to the eternal Brahman. This world is not for the man who does not perform sacrifice; how then can he have the other, O Arjuna? COMMENTARY: They go to the eternal Brahman after attaining knowledge of the Self through purification of the mind by performing the above sacrifices. He who does not perform any of these is not fit even for this miserable world. How then can he hope to get a better world than this? Evam bahuvidhaa yajnaa vitataa brahmano mukhe; Karmajaan viddhi taan sarvaan evam jnaatwaa vimokshyase. 32. Thus, various kinds of sacrifices are spread out before Brahman (literally at the mouth or face of Brahman). Know them all as born of action, and knowing thus, thou shalt be liberated. Shreyaan dravyamayaadyajnaaj jnaanayajnah parantapa; Sarvam karmaakhilam paartha jnaane parisamaapyate. 33. Superior is wisdom-sacrifice to sacrifice with objects, O Parantapa! All actions in their entirety, O Arjuna, culminate in knowledge! Tadviddhi pranipaatena pariprashnena sevayaa; Upadekshyanti te jnaanam jnaaninas tattwadarshinah. 34. Know that by long prostration, by question and by service, the wise who have realised the Truth will instruct thee in (that) knowledge. Yajjnaatwaa na punarmoham evam yaasyasi paandava; 44 THE YOGA OF WISDOM Yena bhootaanyasheshena drakshyasyaatmanyatho mayi. 35. Knowing that, thou shalt not, O Arjuna, again become deluded like this; and by that thou shalt see all beings in thy Self and also in Me! Api chedasi paapebhyah sarvebhyah paapakrittamah; Sarvam jnaanaplavenaiva vrijinam santarishyasi. 36. Even if thou art the most sinful of all sinners, yet thou shalt verily cross all sins by the raft of knowledge. COMMENTARY: One can overcome sin through Self-knowledge. Yathaidhaamsi samiddho'gnir bhasmasaat kurute'rjuna; Jnaanaagnih sarvakarmaani bhasmasaat kurute tathaa. 37. As the blazing fire reduces fuel to ashes, O Arjuna, so does the fire of knowledge reduce all actions to ashes! Na hi jnaanena sadrisham pavitram iha vidyate; Tat swayam yogasamsiddhah kaalenaatmani vindati. 38. Verily there is no purifier in this world like knowledge. He who is perfected in Yoga finds it in the Self in time. Shraddhaavaan labhate jnaanam tatparah samyatendriyah; Jnaanam labdhvaa paraam shaantim achirenaadhigacchati. 39. The man who is full of faith, who is devoted to it, and who has subdued all the senses, obtains (this) knowledge; and, having obtained the knowledge, he goes at once to the supreme peace. Ajnashchaashraddhadhaanashcha samshayaatmaa vinashyati; Naayam loko'sti na paro na sukham samshayaatmanah. 40. The ignorant, the faithless, the doubting self proceeds to destruction; there is neither this world nor the other nor happiness for the doubting. Yogasannyasta karmaanam jnaanasamcchinnasamshayam; Aatmavantam na karmaani nibadhnanti dhananjaya. 41. He who has renounced actions by Yoga, whose doubts are rent asunder by knowledge, and who is self-possessed,—actions do not bind him, O Arjuna! Tasmaad ajnaanasambhootam hritstham jnaanaasinaatmanah; Cchittwainam samshayam yogam aatishthottishtha bhaarata. 45 BHAGAVAD GITA 42. Therefore, with the sword of knowledge (of the Self) cut asunder the doubt of the self born of ignorance, residing in thy heart, and take refuge in Yoga; arise, O Arjuna!

CHAPTER NINE

Summary of Fifth Discourse

In spite of Sri Krishna's clear instructions, Arjuna still seems to be bewildered. He wants to know conclusively which is superior, the path of action or the path of renunciation of action. The Lord says that both the paths lead to the highest goal of God-realisation. In both cases the final realisation of the Atman is the aim, but the path of Karma Yoga is superior. Actually there is no real difference between the two. Krishna further asserts that perfection can be attained and one can be established in the Atman only after the mind has been purified through the performance of selfless action. The Karma Yogi who is aware of the Atman and who is constantly engaged in action knows that although the intellect, mind and senses are active, he does not do anything. He is a spectator of everything. He dedicates all his actions to the Lord and thus abandons attachment, ever remaining pure and unaffected. He surrenders himself completely to the Divine Shakti. Having completely rooted out all desires, attachments and the ego, he is not born again. The sage who has realised Brahman and is always absorbed in It does not have any rebirth. Such a sage sees Brahman within and without—within as the static and transcendent Brahman, and without as the entire universe. He sees the one Self in all beings and creatures—in a cow, an elephant, and even in a dog and an outcaste. He is ever free from joy and grief and enjoys eternal peace and happiness. He does not depend upon the senses for his satisfaction. On the other hand the enjoyments of the senses are generators of pain. They are impermanent. Sri Krishna reminds Arjuna that desire is the main cause of pain and suffering. It is the cause of anger. Therefore, the aspirant should try to eradicate desire and anger if he is to reach the Supreme. The Lord concludes by describing how to control the senses, mind and intellect by concentrating between the eyebrows and practising Pranayama. One who has achieved perfect 46 THE YOGA OF WISDOM control of the outgoing senses and is freed from desire, anger and fear attains liberation and enjoys perfect peace. Arjuna Uvaacha: Sannyaasam karmanaam krishna punar yogam cha shamsasi; Yacchreya etayorekam tanme broohi sunishchitam. Arjuna said: 1. Renunciation of actions, O Krishna, Thou praisest, and again Yoga! Tell me conclusively which is the better of the two. Sri Bhagavaan Uvaacha: Sannyaasah karmayogashcha nihshreyasakaraa vubhau; Tayostu karmasannyaasaat karmayogo vishishyate. The Blessed Lord said: 2. Renunciation and the Yoga of action both lead to the highest bliss; but of the two, the Yoga of action is superior to the renunciation of action. Jneyah sa nityasannyaasi yo na dweshti na kaangkshati; Nirdwandwo hi mahaabaaho sukham bandhaat pramuchyate. 3. He should be known as a perpetual Sannyasin who neither hates nor desires; for, free from the pairs of opposites, O mighty-armed Arjuna, he is easily set free from bondage! COMMENTARY: A man does not become a Sannyasin by merely giving up actions due to laziness, ignorance, some family quarrel or calamity or unemployment. A true Sannyasin is one who has neither attachment nor aversion to anything. Physical renunciation of objects is no renunciation at all. What is wanted is the renunciation of egoism and desires. Saankhyayogau prithagbaalaah pravadanti na panditaah; Ekam apyaasthitah samyag ubhayor vindate phalam. 4. Children, not the wise, speak of knowledge and the Yoga of action or the performance of action as though they are distinct and different; he who is truly established in one obtains the fruits of both. Yatsaankhyaih praapyate sthaanam tad yogair api gamyate; Ekam saankhyam cha yogam cha yah pashyati sa pashyati. 5. That place which is reached by the Sankhyas or the Jnanis is reached by the (Karma) Yogis. He sees who sees knowledge and the performance of action (Karma Yoga) as one. 47 BHAGAVAD GITA Sannyaasastu mahaabaaho duhkham aaptuma yogatah; Yogayukto munir brahma na chirenaadhigacchati. 6. But renunciation, O mighty-armed Arjuna, is hard to attain without Yoga; the Yoga-harmonised sage proceeds quickly to Brahman! Yogayukto vishuddhaatmaa vijitaatmaa jitendriyah; Sarvabhootaatmabhootaatmaa kurvannapi na lipyate. 7. He who is devoted to the path of action, whose mind is quite pure, who has conquered the self, who has subdued his senses and who has realised his Self as the Self in all beings, though acting, he is not tainted. Naiva kinchit karomeeti yukto manyeta tattwavit; Pashyan shrunvan sprishan jighran nashnan gacchan swapan shwasan. 8. "I do nothing at all"—thus will the harmonised knower of Truth think—seeing, hearing, touching, smelling, eating, going, sleeping, breathing, Pralapan visrijan grihnan nunmishan nimishannapi; Indriyaaneendriyaartheshu vartanta iti dhaarayan. 9. Speaking, letting go, seizing, opening and closing the eyes—convinced that the senses move among the sense-objects. COMMENTARY: The liberated sage always remains as a witness of the activities of the senses as he identifies himself with the Self. Brahmanyaadhaaya karmaani sangam tyaktwaa karoti yah; Lipyate na sa paapena padmapatram ivaambhasaa. 10. He who performs actions, offering them to Brahman and abandoning attachment, is not tainted by sin as a lotus leaf by water. Kaayena manasaa buddhyaa kevalair indriyair api; Yoginah karma kurvanti sangam tyaktwaatmashuddhaye. 11. Yogis, having abandoned attachment, perform actions only by the body, mind, intellect and also by the senses, for the purification of the self. Yuktah karmaphalam tyaktwaa shaantim aapnoti naishthikeem; Ayuktah kaamakaarena phale sakto nibadhyate. 12. The united one (the well poised or the harmonised), having abandoned the fruit of action, attains to the eternal peace; the non-united only (the unsteady or the unbalanced), impelled by desire and attached to the fruit, is bound. 48 THE YOGA OF RENUNCIATION OF ACTION Sarvakarmaani manasaa sannyasyaaste sukham vashee; Navadwaare pure dehee naiva kurvan na kaarayan. 13. Mentally renouncing all actions and self-controlled, the embodied one rests happily in the nine-gated city, neither acting nor causing others (body and senses) to act. Na kartritwam na karmaani lokasya srijati prabhuh; Na karmaphala samyogam swabhaavas tu pravartate. 14. Neither agency nor actions does the Lord create for the world, nor union with the fruits of actions; it is Nature that acts. Naadatte kasyachit paapam na chaiva sukritam vibhuh; Ajnaanenaavritam jnaanam tena muhyanti jantavah. 15. The Lord accepts neither the demerit nor even the merit of any; knowledge is enveloped by ignorance, thereby beings are deluded. Jnaanena tu tad ajnaanam yeshaam naashitam aatmanah; Teshaam aadityavaj jnaanam prakaashayati tatparam. 16. But, to those whose ignorance is destroyed by knowledge of the Self, like the sun, knowledge reveals the Supreme (Brahman). Tadbuddhayas tadaatmaanas tannishthaas tatparaayanaah; Gacchantyapunaraavrittim jnaana nirdhoota kalmashaah. 17. Their intellect absorbed in That, their self being That; established in That, with That as their supreme goal, they go whence there is no return, their sins dispelled by knowledge. Vidyaavinaya sampanne braahmane gavi hastini; Shuni chaiva shvapaake cha panditaah samadarshinah. 18. Sages look with an equal eye on a Brahmin endowed with learning and humility, on a cow, on an elephant, and even on a dog and an outcaste. Ihaiva tairjitah sargo yeshaam saamye sthitam manah; Nirdosham hi samam brahma tasmaad brahmani te sthitaah. 19. Even here (in this world) birth (everything) is overcome by those whose minds rest in equality; Brahman is spotless indeed and equal; therefore, they are established in Brahman. Na prahrishyet priyam praapya nodwijet praapya chaapriyam; Sthirabuddhir asammoodho brahmavid brahmani sthitah. 49 BHAGAVAD GITA 20. Resting in Brahman, with steady intellect, undeluded, the knower of Brahman neither rejoiceth on obtaining what is pleasant nor grieveth on obtaining what is unpleasant. Baahyasparsheshwasaktaatmaa vindatyaatmani yat sukham; Sa brahma yoga yuktaatmaa sukham akshayam ashnute. 21. With the self unattached to the external contacts he discovers happiness in the Self; with the self engaged in the meditation of Brahman he attains to the endless happiness. Ye hi samsparshajaa bhogaa duhkhayonaya eva te; Aadyantavantah kaunteya na teshu ramate budhah. 22. The enjoyments that are born of contacts are generators of pain only, for they have a beginning and an end, O Arjuna! The wise do not rejoice in them. Shaknoteehaiva yah sodhum praak shareera vimokshanaat; Kaamakrodhodbhavam vegam sa yuktah sa sukhee narah. 23. He who is able, while still here in this world to withstand, before the liberation from the body, the impulse born of desire and anger—he is a Yogi, he is a happy man. Yo'ntah sukho'ntaraaraamas tathaantarjyotir eva yah; Sa yogee brahma nirvaanam brahmabhooto'dhigacchati. 24. He who is ever happy within, who rejoices within, who is illumined within, such a Yogi attains absolute freedom or Moksha, himself becoming Brahman. Labhante brahma nirvaanam rishayah ksheenakalmashaah; Cchinnadwaidhaa yataatmaanah sarvabhootahite rataah. 25. The sages obtain absolute freedom or Moksha—they whose sins have been destroyed, whose dualities (perception of dualities or experience of the pairs of opposites) are torn asunder, who are self-controlled, and intent on the welfare of all beings. Kaamakrodhaviyuktaanaam yateenaam yatachetasaam; Abhito brahma nirvaanam vartate viditaatmanaam. 26. Absolute freedom (or Brahmic bliss) exists on all sides for those self-controlled ascetics who are free from desire and anger, who have controlled their thoughts and who have realised the Self. Sparsaan kritwaa bahir baahyaamschakshus chaivaantare bhruvoh; Praanaapaanau samau kritwaa naasaabhyantara chaarinau. 27. Shutting out (all) external contacts and fixing the gaze between the eyebrows, equalising the outgoing and incoming breaths moving within the nostrils, 50 THE YOGA OF RENUNCIATION OF ACTION Yatendriya manobuddhir munir mokshaparaayanah; Vigatecchaabhaya krodho yah sadaa mukta eva sah. 28. With the senses, the mind and the intellect always controlled, having liberation as his supreme goal, free from desire, fear and anger—the sage is verily liberated for ever. Bhoktaaram yajnatapasaam sarvaloka maheshwaram; Suhridam sarvabhootaanaam jnaatwaa maam shaantim ricchati. 29. He who knows Me as the enjoyer of sacrifices and austerities, the great Lord of all the worlds and the friend of all beings, attains to peace.

CHAPTER TEN

Summary of Sixth Discourse

Sri Krishna emphasises once again that the Yogi or Sannyasin is one who has renounced the fruits of actions, not the actions themselves. The performance of actions without an eye on their fruits brings about the purification of the mind. Only a purified mind, a mind free from desires, can engage itself in constant meditation on the Atman. Desire gives rise to imagination or Sankalpa, which drives the soul into the field of action. Therefore, none can realise permanent freedom and tranquillity of mind without renouncing desires. The lower self must be controlled by the higher Self. All the lower impulses of the body, mind and senses must be controlled by the power of the higher Self. Then the higher Self becomes one's friend. He who has perfect control of the body, mind and senses and is united with God, sees God in all objects and beings. He sees inwardly that there is no difference between gold and stone, between friends and enemies, between the righteous and the unrighteous. He is perfectly harmonised. Sri Krishna proceeds to give various practical hints as to the practice of meditation. The aspirant should select a secluded spot where there is no likelihood of disturbance. He should arrange his meditation seat properly and sit in a comfortable posture, with the head, neck and spine 51 BHAGAVAD GITA erect but not tensed. He should fix his purified mind on the Atman by concentrating between the eyebrows or on the tip of the nose. The practice of Brahmacharya is absolutely necessary if one is to succeed in meditation. The conservation and transformation of the vital fluid into spiritual energy gives immense power of concentration. Fearlessness, too, is an essential quality on the Godward path. It is faith in the sustaining protection and Grace of God. The aspirant is advised to practise moderation in his daily habits—in eating, sleeping, recreation, etc. Extremes are to be avoided as they hinder the practice of meditation. Living a life of such moderation, and gathering up all his forces and directing them towards meditation upon the Atman, the aspirant gradually transcends the senses and intellect and merges himself in the blissful Atman. He finds that the bliss of the Atman is incomparable, that there is no gain greater than the Self. Having thus attained perfect union with the Self, the Yogi no more descends into ignorance or delusion. He does not relish any more the pleasures of the senses. Lord Krishna again emphasises that the concentration of the mind on the Atman should be like a steady flame in a windless place. This ultimately leads to the vision of the Lord in all beings and creatures. Arjuna is doubtful whether it is at all possible to engage the mind steadily on the higher Self, as its very nature seems to be one of restlessness. Krishna assures him that the practice can succeed through Vairagya (dispassion) and constant effort. Arjuna wishes to know the fate of the aspirant who fails to realise the Supreme in spite of his faith and sincerity. Krishna tells him that the accumulated power of his Yogic practices will assure him a better birth in the future, with more favourable conditions for Sadhana. The aspirant will then be compelled to carry on his Yogic practices with greater vigour and faith and will finally achieve God-realisation. Krishna concludes that the Yogi—one who has attained union with the Supreme Lord—is superior to the ascetics, to the men of book knowledge and the men of action, as the latter have not transcended ignorance and merged in the Self. Sri Bhagavaan Uvaacha: Anaashritah karmaphalam kaaryam karma karoti yah; Sa sannyaasi cha yogee cha na niragnirna chaakriyah. The Blessed Lord said: 1. He who performs his bounden duty without depending on the fruits of his actions—he is a Sannyasin and a Yogi, not he who is without fire and without action. Yam sannyaasamiti praahuryogam tam viddhi paandava; Na hyasannyastasankalpo yogee bhavati kashchana. 52 THE YOGA OF MEDITATION 2. Do thou, O Arjuna, know Yoga to be that which they call renunciation; no one verily becomes a Yogi who has not renounced thoughts! COMMENTARY: Lord Krishna eulogises Karma Yoga here because it is a means or a stepping stone to the Yoga of meditation. In order to encourage the practice of Karma Yoga it is stated here that it is Sannyasa. Aarurukshormuneryogam karma kaaranamuchyate; Yogaaroodhasya tasyaiva shamah kaaranamuchyate. 3. For a sage who wishes to attain to Yoga, action is said to be the means; for the same sage who has attained to Yoga, inaction (quiescence) is said to be the means. Yadaa hi nendriyaartheshu na karmaswanushajjate; Sarvasankalpasannyaasee yogaaroodhas tadochyate. 4. When a man is not attached to the sense-objects or to actions, having renounced all thoughts, then he is said to have attained to Yoga. Uddharedaatmanaatmaanam naatmaanamavasaadayet; Atmaiva hyaatmano bandhuraatmaiva ripuraatmanah. 5. Let a man lift himself by his own Self alone; let him not lower himself, for this self alone is the friend of oneself and this self alone is the enemy of oneself. Bandhuraatmaa'tmanastasya yenaatmaivaatmanaa jitah; Anaatmanastu shatrutwe vartetaatmaiva shatruvat. 6. The self is the friend of the self for him who has conquered himself by the Self, but to the unconquered self, this self stands in the position of an enemy like the (external) foe. Jitaatmanah prashaantasya paramaatmaa samaahitah; Sheetoshna sukha duhkheshu tathaa maanaapamaanayoh. 7. The Supreme Self of him who is self-controlled and peaceful is balanced in cold and heat, pleasure and pain, as also in honour and dishonour. Jnaana vijnaana triptaatmaa kootastho vijitendriyah; Yuktah ityuchyate yogee samaloshtaashmakaanchanah. 8. The Yogi who is satisfied with the knowledge and the wisdom (of the Self), who has conquered the senses, and to whom a clod of earth, a piece of stone and gold are the same, is said to be harmonised (that is, is said to have attained the state of Nirvikalpa Samadhi). Suhrinmitraary udaaseena madhyastha dweshya bandhushu; Saadhushwapi cha paapeshu samabuddhirvishishyate. 53 BHAGAVAD GITA 9. He who is of the same mind to the good-hearted, friends, enemies, the indifferent, the neutral, the hateful, the relatives, the righteous and the unrighteous, excels. Yogee yunjeeta satatamaatmaanam rahasi sthitah; Ekaakee yatachittaatmaa niraasheeraparigrahah. 10. Let the Yogi try constantly to keep the mind steady, remaining in solitude, alone, with the mind and the body controlled, and free from hope and greed. Shuchau deshe pratishthaapya sthiramaasanamaatmanah; Naatyucchritam naatineecham chailaajinakushottaram. 11. In a clean spot, having established a firm seat of his own, neither too high nor too low, made of a cloth, a skin and kusha grass, one over the other, Tatraikaagram manah kritwaa yatachittendriyakriyah; Upavishyaasane yunjyaadyogamaatmavishuddhaye. 12. There, having made the mind one-pointed, with the actions of the mind and the senses controlled, let him, seated on the seat, practise Yoga for the purification of the self. Samam kaayashirogreevam dhaarayannachalam sthirah; Samprekshya naasikaagram swam dishashchaanavalokayan. 13. Let him firmly hold his body, head and neck erect and perfectly still, gazing at the tip of his nose, without looking around. Prashaantaatmaa vigatabheer brahmachaarivrate sthitah; Manah samyamya macchitto yukta aaseeta matparah. 14. Sereneminded, fearless, firm in the vow of a Brahmachari, having controlled the mind, thinking of Me and balanced in mind, let him sit, having Me as his supreme goal. Yunjannevam sadaa'tmaanam yogee niyatamaanasah; Shaantim nirvaanaparamaam matsamsthaamadhigacchati. 15. Thus, always keeping the mind balanced, the Yogi, with the mind controlled, attains to the peace abiding in Me, which culminates in liberation. Naatyashnatastu yogo'sti nachaikaantamanashnatah; Na chaatiswapnasheelasya jaagrato naiva chaarjuna. 16. Verily Yoga is not possible for him who eats too much, nor for him who does not eat at all; nor for him who sleeps too much, nor for him who is (always) awake, O Arjuna! Yuktaahaaravihaarasya yuktacheshtasya karmasu; 54 THE YOGA OF MEDITATION Yuktaswapnaavabodhasya yogo bhavati duhkhahaa. 17. Yoga becomes the destroyer of pain for him who is always moderate in eating and recreation (such as walking, etc.), who is moderate in exertion in actions, who is moderate in sleep and wakefulness. Yadaa viniyatam chittamaatmanyevaavatishthate; Nihsprihah sarvakaamebhyo yukta ityuchyate tadaa. 18. When the perfectly controlled mind rests in the Self only, free from longing for the objects of desire, then it is said: "He is united." COMMENTARY: Without union with the Self neither harmony nor balance nor Samadhi is possible. Yathaa deepo nivaatastho nengate sopamaa smritaa; Yogino yatachittasya yunjato yogamaatmanah. 19. As a lamp placed in a windless spot does not flicker—to such is compared the Yogi of controlled mind, practising Yoga in the Self (or absorbed in the Yoga of the Self). COMMENTARY: This is a beautiful simile which Yogis often quote when they talk of concentration or one-pointedness of mind. Yatroparamate chittam niruddham yogasevayaa; Yatra chaivaatmanaa'tmaanam pashyannaatmani tushyati. 20. When the mind, restrained by the practice of Yoga, attains to quietude, and when, seeing the Self by the Self, he is satisfied in his own Self, Sukhamaatyantikam yattad buddhi graahyamateendriyam; Vetti yatra na chaivaayam sthitashchalati tattwatah. 21. When he (the Yogi) feels that infinite bliss which can be grasped by the (pure) intellect and which transcends the senses, and, established wherein he never moves from the Reality, Yam labdhwaa chaaparam laabham manyate naadhikam tatah; Yasmin sthito na duhkhena gurunaapi vichaalyate. 22. Which, having obtained, he thinks there is no other gain superior to it; wherein established, he is not moved even by heavy sorrow,— Tam vidyaad duhkhasamyogaviyogam yogasamjnitam; Sa nishchayena yoktavyo yogo'nirvinna chetasaa. 55 BHAGAVAD GITA 23.

Let that be known by the name of Yoga, the severance from union with pain. This Yoga should be practised with determination and with an undesponding mind. Sankalpaprabhavaan kaamaan styaktwaa sarvaan asheshatah; Manasaivendriyagraamam viniyamya samantatah. 24. Abandoning without reserve all the desires born of Sankalpa, and completely restraining the whole group of senses by the mind from all sides, COMMENTARY: The mind is so diplomatic that it keeps certain desires for its secret gratification. So one should completely abandon all desires without reservation. Shanaih shanairuparamed buddhyaa dhritigriheetayaa; Aatmasamstham manah kritwaa na kinchidapi chintayet. 25. Little by little let him attain to quietude by the intellect held firmly; having made the mind establish itself in the Self, let him not think of anything. Yato yato nishcharati manashchanchalamasthiram; Tatastato niyamyaitad aatmanyeva vasham nayet. 26. From whatever cause the restless, unsteady mind wanders away, from that let him restrain it and bring it under the control of the Self alone. Prashaantamanasam hyenam yoginam sukhamuttamam; Upaiti shaantarajasam brahmabhootamakalmasham. 27. Supreme bliss verily comes to this Yogi whose mind is quite peaceful, whose passion is quieted, who has become Brahman, and who is free from sin. Yunjannevam sadaa'tmaanam yogee vigatakalmashah; Sukhena brahmasamsparsham atyantam sukham ashnute. 28. The Yogi, always engaging the mind thus (in the practice of Yoga), freed from sins, easily enjoys the infinite bliss of contact with Brahman (the Eternal). Sarvabhootasthamaatmaanam sarvabhootaani chaatmani; Eekshate yogayuktaatmaa sarvatra samadarshanah. 29. With the mind harmonised by Yoga he sees the Self abiding in all beings and all beings in the Self; he sees the same everywhere. Yo maam pashyati sarvatra sarvam cha mayi pashyati; Tasyaaham na pranashyaami sa cha me na pranashyati. 56 THE YOGA OF MEDITATION 30. He who sees Me everywhere and sees everything in Me, he does not become separated from Me nor do I become separated from him. COMMENTARY: The Lord describes here the effect of oneness. Sarvabhootasthitam yo maam bhajatyekatwamaasthitah; Sarvathaa vartamaano'pi sa yogee mayi vartate. 31. He who, being established in unity, worships Me who dwells in all beings,—that Yogi abides in Me, whatever may be his mode of living. Aatmaupamyena sarvatra samam pashyati yo'rjuna; Sukham vaa yadi vaa duhkham sa yogee paramo matah. 32. He who, through the likeness of the Self, O Arjuna, sees equality everywhere, be it pleasure or pain, he is regarded as the highest Yogi! Arjuna Uvaacha:

Yo'yam yogastwayaa proktah saamyena madhusoodana; Etasyaaham na pashyaami chanchalatwaat sthitim sthiraam. Arjuna said: 33. This Yoga of equanimity taught by Thee, O Krishna, I do not see its steady continuance, because of restlessness (of the mind)! Chanchalam hi manah krishna pramaathi balavad dridham; Tasyaaham nigraham manye vaayoriva sudushkaram. 34. The mind verily is restless, turbulent, strong and unyielding, O Krishna! I deem it as difficult to control as to control the wind. COMMENTARY: The mind ever changes its point of concentration from one object to another. So it is always restless. It is not only restless but also turbulent and impetuous, strong and obstinate. It produces agitation in the body and in the senses. That is why the mind is even more difficult to control than to control the wind. Sri Bhagavaan Uvaacha: Asamshayam mahaabaaho mano durnigraham chalam; Abhyaasena tu kaunteya vairaagyena cha grihyate. The Blessed Lord said: 35. Undoubtedly, O mighty-armed Arjuna, the mind is difficult to control and restless; but, by practice and by dispassion it may be restrained! 57 BHAGAVAD GITA Asamyataatmanaa yogo dushpraapa iti me matih; Vashyaatmanaa tu yatataa shakyo'vaaptumupaayatah. 36. I think that Yoga is hard to be attained by one of uncontrolled self, but the self~controlled and striving one attains to it by the (proper) means. Arjuna Uvaacha: Ayatih shraddhayopeto yogaacchalitamaanasah; Apraapya yogasamsiddhim kaam gatim krishna gacchati. Arjuna said: 37. He who is unable to control himself though he has the faith, and whose mind wanders away from Yoga, what end does he meet, having failed to attain perfection in Yoga, O Krishna? Kacchinnobhayavibhrashtash cchinnaabhramiva nashyati; Apratishtho mahaabaaho vimoodho brahmanah pathi. 38. Fallen from both, does he not perish like a rent cloud, supportless, O mighty-armed (Krishna), deluded on the path of Brahman? Etanme samshayam krishna cchettumarhasyasheshatah; Twadanyah samshayasyaasya cchettaa na hyupapadyate. 39. This doubt of mine, O Krishna, do Thou completely dispel, because it is not possible for any but Thee to dispel this doubt. COMMENTARY: There is no better teacher than the Lord Himself as He is omniscient. Sri Bhagavaan Uvaacha: Paartha naiveha naamutra vinaashas tasya vidyate; Nahi kalyaanakrit kashchid durgatim taata gacchati. The Blessed Lord said: 40. O Arjuna, neither in this world, nor in the next world is there destruction for him; none, verily, who does good, O My son, ever comes to grief! Praapya punyakritaam lokaanushitwaa shaashwateeh samaah; Shucheenaam shreemataam gehe yogabhrashto'bhijaayate. 41.

Having attained to the worlds of the righteous and, having dwelt there for everlasting years, he who fell from Yoga is reborn in the house of the pure and wealthy. Athavaa yoginaameva kule bhavati dheemataam; Etaddhi durlabhataram loke janma yadeedrisham. 58 THE YOGA OF MEDITATION 42. Or he is born in a family of even the wise Yogis; verily a birth like this is very difficult to obtain in this world. Tatra tam buddhisamyogam labhate paurvadehikam; Yatate cha tato bhooyah samsiddhau kurunandana. 43. There he comes in touch with the knowledge acquired in his former body and strives more than before for perfection, O Arjuna! Poorvaabhyaasena tenaiva hriyate hyavasho'pi sah; Jijnaasurapi yogasya shabdabrahmaativartate. 44. By that very former practice he is borne on in spite of himself. Even he who merely wishes to know Yoga transcends the Brahmic word. COMMENTARY: One who had fallen from Yoga is carried to the goal (which he intended to reach in his previous birth), by the force of the impressions of his past Yogic practices, though he may be unconscious of it and may not be willing to adopt the course of Yogic discipline due to the force of some evil Karma. Prayatnaadyatamaanastu yogee samshuddhakilbishah; Anekajanmasamsiddhas tato yaati paraam gatim. 45. But, the Yogi who strives with assiduity, purified of sins and perfected gradually through many births, reaches the highest goal. Tapaswibhyo'dhiko yogee jnaanibhyo'pi mato'dhikah; Karmibhyashchaadhiko yogee tasmaad yogee bhavaarjuna. 46. The Yogi is thought to be superior to the ascetics and even superior to men of knowledge (obtained through the study of scriptures); he is also superior to men of action; therefore, be thou a Yogi, O Arjuna! Yoginaamapi sarveshaam madgatenaantaraatmanaa; Shraddhaavaan bhajate yo maam sa me yuktatamo matah. 47. And among all the Yogis, he who, full of faith and with his inner self merged in Me, worships Me, he is deemed by Me to be the most devout. Hari Om Tat Sat Iti Srimad Bhagavadgeetaasoopanishatsu Brahmavidyaayaam Yogashaastre Sri Krishnaarjunasamvaade Aatmasamyamayogo Naama Shashtho'dhyaayah

CHAPTER ELEVEN

WISDOM AND REALISATION
Summary of Seventh Discourse

Sri Krishna tells Arjuna that the supreme Godhead has to be realised in both its transcendent and immanent aspects. The Yogi who has reached this summit has nothing more to know. This complete union with the Lord is difficult of attainment. Among many thousands of human beings, very few aspire for this union, and even among those who aspire for it, few ever reach the pinnacle of spiritual realisation. The Lord has already given a clear description of the all-pervading static and infinite state of His. Now He proceeds to explain His manifestations as the universe and the power behind it. He speaks of these manifestations as His lower and higher Prakritis. The lower Prakriti is made up of the five elements, mind, ego and intellect. The higher Prakriti is the life-element which upholds the universe, activates it and causes its appearance and final dissolution. Krishna says that whatever exists is nothing but Himself. He is the cause of the appearance of the universe and all things in it. Everything is strung on Him like clusters of gems on a string. He is the essence, substance and substratum of everything, whether visible or invisible. Although everything is in Him, yet He transcends everything as the actionless Self. Prakriti or Nature is made up of the three Gunas or qualities—Sattwa, Rajas and Tamas. These three qualities delude the soul and make it forget its true nature, which is one with God. This delusion, termed Maya, can only be removed by the Grace of the Lord Himself. Thus far Arjuna has been taught the highest form of devotion, which leads to union with God in His static aspect as also with His dynamic Prakriti. Krishna tells him that there are also other forms of devotion which are inferior as they are performed with various motives. The distressed, the seeker of divine wisdom, and he who desires wealth, worship Him, as also the wise. Of these the Lord deems the wise as dearest to Him. Such a devotee loves the Lord for the sake of pure love alone. Whatever form the devotee worships, the ultimate goal is the Lord Himself. The Lord accepts such worship, knowing that it is directed to Him only. Sri Bhagavaan Uvaacha: Mayyaasaktamanaah paartha yogam yunjanmadaashrayah; Asamshayam samagram maam yathaa jnaasyasi tacchrinu. 60 THE YOGA OF MEDITATION The Blessed Lord said: 1. O Arjuna, hear how you shall without doubt know Me fully, with the mind intent on Me, practising Yoga and taking refuge in Me! COMMENTARY: If you sing the glories and attributes of the Lord, you will develop love for Him and then your mind will be ever fixed on Him. Intense love for the Lord is real devotion. With this you must surely get full knowledge of the Self. Jnaanam te'ham savijnaanam idam vakshyaamyasheshatah; Yajjnaatwaa neha bhooyo'nyaj jnaatavyamavashishyate. 2. I shall declare to thee in full this knowledge combined with direct realisation, after knowing which nothing more here remains to be known. Manushyaanaam sahasreshu kashchidyatati siddhaye; Yataataamapi siddhaanaam kashchinmaam vetti tattwatah. 3. Among thousands of men, one perchance strives for perfection; even among those successful strivers, only one perchance knows Me in essence. Bhoomiraapo'nalo vaayuh kham mano buddhireva cha; Ahamkaara iteeyam me bhinnaa prakritirashtadhaa. 4. Earth, water, fire, air, ether, mind, intellect and egoism—thus is My Nature divided eightfold. Apareyamitastwanyaam prakritim viddhi me paraam; Jeevabhootaam mahaabaaho yayedam dhaaryate jagat. 5. This is the inferior Prakriti, O mighty-armed (Arjuna)! Know thou as different from it My higher Prakriti (Nature), the very life-element by which this world is upheld. Etadyoneeni bhootaani sarvaaneetyupadhaaraya; Aham kritsnasya jagatah prabhavah pralayastathaa. 6. Know that these two (My higher and lower Natures) are the womb of all beings. So, I am the source and dissolution of the whole universe. Mattah parataram naanyat kinchidasti dhananjaya; Mayi sarvamidam protam sootre maniganaa iva. 7. There is nothing whatsoever higher than Me, O Arjuna! All this is strung on Me as clusters of gems on a string. 61 BHAGAVAD GITA COMMENTARY: There is no other cause of the universe but Me. I alone am the cause of the universe. Raso'hamapsu kaunteya prabhaasmi shashisooryayoh; Pranavah sarvavedeshu shabdah khe paurusham nrishu. 8. I am the sapidity in water, O Arjuna! I am the light in the moon and the sun; I am the syllable Om in all the Vedas, sound in ether, and virility in men. Punyo gandhah prithivyaam cha tejashchaasmi vibhaavasau; Jeevanam sarvabhooteshu tapashchaasmi tapaswishu. 9. I am the sweet fragrance in earth and the brilliance in fire, the life in all beings; and I am austerity in ascetics. Beejam maam sarvabhootaanaam viddhi paartha sanaatanam; Buddhir buddhimataamasmi tejastejaswinaamaham. 10. Know Me, O Arjuna, as the eternal seed of all beings; I am the intelligence of the intelligent; the splendour of the splendid objects am I! Balam balavataam asmi kaamaraagavivarjitam; Dharmaaviruddho bhooteshu kaamo'smi bharatarshabha. 11. Of the strong, I am the strength devoid of desire and attachment, and in (all) beings, I am the desire unopposed to Dharma, O Arjuna! Ye chaiva saattvikaa bhaavaa raajasaastaamasaashcha ye; Matta eveti taanviddhi na twaham teshu te mayi. 12. Whatever being (and objects) that are pure, active and inert, know that they proceed from Me. They are in Me, yet I am not in them. Tribhirgunamayair bhaavairebhih sarvamidam jagat; Mohitam naabhijaanaati maamebhyah paramavyayam. 13. Deluded by these Natures (states or things) composed of the three qualities of Nature, all this world does not know Me as distinct from them and immutable. Daivee hyeshaa gunamayee mama maayaa duratyayaa; Maameva ye prapadyante maayaametaam taranti te. 14. Verily this divine illusion of Mine made up of the qualities (of Nature) is difficult to cross over; those who take refuge in Me alone cross over this illusion. Na maam dushkritino moodhaah prapadyante naraadhamaah; 62 THE YOGA OF WISDOM AND REALISATION Maayayaapahritajnaanaa aasuram bhaavamaashritaah. 15. The evil-doers and the deluded, who are the lowest of men, do not seek Me; they whose knowledge is destroyed by illusion follow the ways of demons. Chaturvidhaa bhajante maam janaah sukritino'rjuna; Aarto jijnaasurartharthee jnaanee cha bharatarshabha. 16. Four kinds of virtuous men worship Me, O Arjuna! They are the distressed, the seeker of knowledge, the seeker of wealth, and the wise, O lord of the Bharatas! Teshaam jnaanee nityayukta eka bhaktirvishishyate; Priyo hi jnaanino'tyarthamaham sa cha mama priyah. 17. Of them, the wise, ever steadfast and devoted to the One, excels (is the best); for, I am exceedingly dear to the wise and he is dear to Me. Udaaraah sarva evaite jnaanee twaatmaiva me matam; Aasthitah sa hi yuktaatmaa maamevaanuttamaam gatim. 18. Noble indeed are all these; but I deem the wise man as My very

Self; for, steadfast in mind, he is established in Me alone as the supreme goal. Bahoonaam janmanaamante jnaanavaanmaam prapadyate; Vaasudevah sarvamiti sa mahaatmaa sudurlabhah. 19. At the end of many births the wise man comes to Me, realising that all this is Vasudeva (the innermost Self); such a great soul (Mahatma) is very hard to find. Kaamaistaistairhritajnaanaah prapadyante'nyadevataah; Tam tam niyamamaasthaaya prakrityaa niyataah swayaa. 20. Those whose wisdom has been rent away by this or that desire, go to other gods, following this or that rite, led by their own nature. Yo yo yaam yaam tanum bhaktah shraddhayaarchitum icchati; Tasya tasyaachalaam shraddhaam taameva vidadhaamyaham. 21. Whatsoever form any devotee desires to worship with faith—that (same) faith of his I make firm and unflinching. Sa tayaa shraddhayaa yuktastasyaaraadhanameehate; Labhate cha tatah kaamaan mayaiva vihitaan hi taan. 22. Endowed with that faith, he engages in the worship of that (form), and from it he obtains his desire, these being verily ordained by Me (alone). 63 BHAGAVAD GITA Antavattu phalam teshaam tadbhavatyalpamedhasaam; Devaan devayajo yaanti madbhaktaa yaanti maamapi. 23. Verily the reward (fruit) that accrues to those men of small intelligence is finite. The worshippers of the gods go to them, but My devotees come to Me. Avyaktam vyaktimaapannam manyante maamabuddhayah; Param bhaavamajaananto mamaavyayamanuttamam. 24. The foolish think of Me, the Unmanifest, as having manifestation, knowing not My higher, immutable and most excellent nature. Naaham prakaashah sarvasya yogamaayaasamaavritah; Moodho'yam naabhijaanaati loko maamajamavyayam. 25. I am not manifest to all (as I am), being veiled by the Yoga Maya. This deluded world does not know Me, the unborn and imperishable. Vedaaham samateetaani vartamaanaani chaarjuna; Bhavishyaani cha bhootani maam tu veda na kashchana. 26. I know, O Arjuna, the beings of the past, the present and the future, but no one knows Me. Icchaadweshasamutthena dwandwamohena bhaarata; Sarvabhootaani sammoham sarge yaanti parantapa. 27. By the delusion of the pairs of opposites arising from desire and aversion, O Bharata, all beings are subject to delusion at birth, O Parantapa! Yeshaam twantagatam paapam janaanaam punyakarmanaam; Te dwandwamohanirmuktaa bhajante maam dridhavrataah. 28. But those men of virtuous deeds whose sins have come to an end, and who are freed from the delusion of the pairs of opposites, worship Me, steadfast in their vows. Jaraamaranamokshaaya maamaashritya yatanti ye; Te brahma tadviduh kritsnam adhyaatmam karma chaakhilam.

29. Those who strive for liberation from old age and death, taking refuge in Me, realise in full that Brahman, the whole knowledge of the Self and all action. Saadhibhootaadhidaivam maam saadhiyajnam cha ye viduh; Prayaanakaale'pi cha maam te vidur yuktachetasah. 64 THE YOGA OF WISDOM AND REALISATION 30. Those who know Me with the Adhibhuta (pertaining to the elements), the Adhidaiva (pertaining to the gods), and Adhiyajna (pertaining to the sacrifice), know Me even at the time of death, steadfast in mind. COMMENTARY: They who are steadfast in mind, who have taken refuge in Me, who know Me as knowledge of elements on the physical plane, as knowledge of gods on the celestial or mental plane, as knowledge of sacrifice in the realm of sacrifice,—they are not affected by death.

CHAPTER TWELVE

IMPERISHABLE BRAHMAN
Summary of Eighth Discourse

Lord Krishna explains how those who attain Him do not have to come again into this impermanent world of sorrow and pain. All beings, including even the gods, come again and again into this created universe from the state of unmanifest being wherein they remained at the end of an age-cycle. But the Lord exists even beyond this unmanifest being. That radiant, imperishable Divine Reality is the highest goal to be attained. Single-minded devotion of our heart is the means of attaining this highest blessed state. Even though there are auspicious and inauspicious circumstances of departing from the physical body and journeying forth, yet if one steadily abides in the Lord through firm devotion and faith, then these conditions do not matter. By always remaining in tune with the Lord through pure love, everything is made auspicious, if one can ever remain united with the Divine through deep devotion, constant remembrance, regular meditation and continuous communion, then all times, places, conditions and situations become auspicious and blessed. This is the secret of invoking His Grace and attaining Him and becoming eternally free and blissful. Arjuna here asks Lord Krishna about the meaning of the different terms referred to by Him in the last two verses of the previous chapter. He wishes to know what is the Supreme Being, what is Karma or action that He refers to, and what is the meaning that pertains to this spirit, the elements and the centre of all things within this human body. Beyond all things manifest and unmanifest, beyond these names and forms, there is the Supreme Being—Brahman. He indwells this body as the centre of all things, including even our own self (individual soul). We are a spiritual being residing in this body and supported by the Silent Witness within—the Supreme Antaryamin. Prakriti or Nature is the being pertaining to the elements. Worship, prayer and offering to the gods with faith and devotion constitute actions that lead to blessedness. The secret of reaching the Divine Being and thus freeing oneself forever from birth and death and the pains and sufferings of this earth-life, is to constantly practise unbroken remembrance of the Lord at all times, in all places and even amidst one's daily activities. If one practises such steady remembrance through regular daily Sadhana, then he will be rooted in His remembrance even at the time of departing from this body at death. Thus departing, he will go beyond darkness and bondage and attain the realm of eternal blessedness. One must practise sense-control. The senses must be well disciplined and gradually withdrawn from outside objects. The mind should be centred within upon God, by uttering Om or any Divine Name. By such steady practice daily the Lord is easily attained.

Arjuna Uvaacha: Kim tadbrahma kim adhyaatmam kim karma purushottama; Adhibhootam cha kim proktam adhidaivam kimuchyate. Arjuna said: 1. What is that Brahman? What is Adhyatma? What is action, O best among men? What is declared to be Adhibhuta? And what is Adhidaiva said to be? Adhiyajnah katham ko'tra dehe'smin madhusoodana; Prayaanakaale cha katham jneyo'si niyataatmabhih. 2. Who and how is Adhiyajna here in this body, O destroyer of Madhu (Krishna)? And how, at the time of death, art Thou to be known by the self-controlled one? COMMENTARY: In the last two verses of the seventh discourse, Lord Krishna uses certain philosophical terms. Arjuna does not understand their meaning. So he proceeds to question the Lord. Sri Bhagavaan Uvaacha: Aksharam brahma paramam swabhaavo'dhyaatmamuchyate; Bhootabhaavodbhavakaro visargah karmasamjnitah. The Blessed Lord said: 66 THE YOGA OF THE IMPERISHABLE BRAHMAN 3. Brahman is the Imperishable, the Supreme; His essential nature is called Self-knowledge; the offering (to the gods) which causes existence and manifestation of beings and which also sustains them is called action. Adhibhootam ksharo bhaavah purushashchaadhidaivatam; Adhiyajno'hamevaatra dehe dehabhritaam vara. 4. Adhibhuta (knowledge of the elements) pertains to My perishable Nature, and the Purusha or soul is the Adhidaiva; I alone am the Adhiyajna here in this body, O best among the embodied (men)! Antakaale cha maameva smaran muktwaa kalevaram; Yah prayaati sa madbhaavam yaati naastyatra samshayah. 5. And whosoever, leaving the body, goes forth remembering Me alone at the time of death, he attains My Being; there is no doubt about this. Yam yam vaapi smaran bhaavam tyajatyante kalevaram; Tam tamevaiti kaunteya sadaa tadbhaavabhaavitah.

6. Whosoever at the end leaves the body, thinking of any being, to that being only does he go, O son of Kunti (Arjuna), because of his constant thought of that being! COMMENTARY: The most prominent thought of one's life occupies the mind at the time of death. It determines the nature of the body to be attained in the next birth. Tasmaat sarveshu kaaleshu maamanusmara yudhya cha; Mayyarpitamanobuddhir maamevaishyasyasamshayam. 7. Therefore, at all times remember Me only and fight. With mind and intellect fixed (or absorbed) in Me, thou shalt doubtless come to Me alone. Abhyaasayogayuktena chetasaa naanyagaaminaa; Paramam purusham divyam yaati paarthaanuchintayan. 8. With the mind not moving towards any other thing, made steadfast by the method of habitual meditation, and constantly meditating, one goes to the Supreme Person, the Resplendent, O Arjuna! Kavim puraanamanushaasitaaram Anoraneeyaamsam anusmaredyah; Sarvasya dhaataaram achintyaroopam Aadityavarnam tamasah parastaat. 67 BHAGAVAD GITA 9. Whosoever meditates on the Omniscient, the Ancient, the ruler (of the whole world), minuter than an atom, the supporter of all, of inconceivable form, effulgent like the sun and beyond the darkness of ignorance, Prayaanakaale manasaachalena Bhaktyaa yukto yogabalena chaiva; Bhruvormadhye praanamaaveshya samyak Sa tam param purusham upaiti divyam. 10. At the time of death, with unshaken mind, endowed with devotion and by the power of Yoga, fixing the whole life-breath in the middle of the two eyebrows, he reaches that resplendent Supreme Person. Yadaksharam vedavido vadanti Vishanti yadyatayo veetaraagaah; Yadicchanto brahmacharyam charanti Tatte padam samgrahena pravakshye. 11. That which is declared imperishable by those who know the Vedas, that which the self-controlled (ascetics) and passion-free enter, that desiring which celibacy is practised—that goal I will declare to thee in brief. Sarvadwaaraani samyamya mano hridi nirudhya cha; Moordhnyaadhaayaatmanah praanamaasthito yogadhaaranaam. 12. Having closed all the gates, confined the mind in the heart and fixed the life-breath in the head, engaged in the practice of concentration, Omityekaaksharam brahma vyaaharan maamanusmaran; Yah prayaati tyajan deham sa yaati paramaam gatim. 13. Uttering the monosyllable Om—the Brahman—remembering Me always, he who departs thus, leaving the body, attains to the supreme goal. Ananyachetaah satatam yo maam smarati nityashah; Tasyaaham sulabhah paartha nityayuktasya yoginah. 14. I am easily attainable by that ever-steadfast Yogi who constantly and daily

remembers Me (for a long time), not thinking of anything else (with a single or one-pointed mind), O Partha (Arjuna)! COMMENTARY: Constantly remembering the Lord throughout one's life is the easiest way of attaining Him. Maamupetya punarjanma duhkhaalayamashaashwatam; Naapnuvanti mahaatmaanah samsiddhim paramaam gataah. 68 THE YOGA OF THE IMPERISHABLE BRAHMAN 15. Having attained Me these great souls do not again take birth (here), which is the place of pain and is non-eternal; they have reached the highest perfection (liberation). Aabrahmabhuvanaallokaah punaraavartino'rjuna; Maamupetya tu kaunteya punarjanma na vidyate. 16. (All) the worlds, including the world of Brahma, are subject to return again, O Arjuna! But he who reaches Me, O son of Kunti, has no rebirth! Sahasrayugaparyantam aharyad brahmano viduh; Raatrim yugasahasraantaam te'horaatravido janaah. 17. Those who know the day of Brahma, which is of a duration of a thousand Yugas (ages), and the night, which is also of a thousand Yugas' duration, they know day and night. Avyaktaadvyaktayah sarvaah prabhavantyaharaagame; Raatryaagame praleeyante tatraivaavyaktasamjnake. 18. From the unmanifested all the manifested (worlds) proceed at the coming of the "day"; at the coming of the "night" they dissolve verily into that alone which is called the unmanifested. COMMENTARY: Coming of the "day' is the commencement of creation. Coming of the "night" is the commencement of dissolution. Bhootagraamah sa evaayam bhootwaa bhootwaa praleeyate; Raatryaagame'vashah paartha prabhavatyaharaagame. 19. This same multitude of beings, born again and again, is dissolved, helplessly, O Arjuna, (into the unmanifested) at the coming of the night, and comes forth at the coming of the day! Parastasmaat tu bhaavo'nyo'vyakto'vyaktaatsanaatanah; Yah sa sarveshu bhooteshu nashyatsu na vinashyati. 20. But verily there exists, higher than the unmanifested, another unmanifested Eternal who is not destroyed when all beings are destroyed. COMMENTARY: Another unmanifested Eternal refers to Para Brahman, which is distinct from the unmanifested (primordial Nature), and which is of quite a different nature. It is superior to Hiranyagarbha (the creative Intelligence) and the unmanifested Nature because It is their cause. It is not destroyed when all beings from Brahma down to a blade of grass are destroyed. Avyakto'kshara ityuktastamaahuh paramaam gatim; Yam praapya na nivartante taddhaama paramam mama. 69 BHAGAVAD GITA 21. What is called the Unmanifested and the Imperishable, That they say is the highest goal (path). They who reach It do not return (to this cycle of births and deaths). That is My highest abode (place or state). Purushah sa parah paartha bhaktyaa labhyastwananyayaa; Yasyaantahsthaani bhootaani yena sarvamidam tatam. 22. That highest Purusha, O Arjuna, is attainable by unswerving devotion to Him alone within whom all beings dwell and by whom all this is pervaded. Yatra kaale twanaavrittim aavrittim chaiva yoginah; Prayaataa yaanti tam kaalam vakshyaami bharatarshabha. 23. Now I will tell thee, O chief of the Bharatas, the times departing at which the Yogis will return or not return! Agnijyotirahah shuklah shanmaasaa uttaraayanam; Tatra prayaataa gacchanti brahma brahmavido janaah. 24. Fire, light, daytime, the bright fortnight, the six months of the northern path of the sun (northern solstice)—departing then (by these), men who know Brahman go to Brahman. Dhoomo raatristathaa krishnah shanmaasaa dakshinaayanam; Tatra chaandramasam jyotir yogee praapya nivartate. 25. Attaining to the lunar light by smoke, night-time, the dark fortnight or the six months of the southern path of the sun (the southern solstice), the Yogi returns. Shuklakrishne gatee hyete jagatah shaashwate mate; Ekayaa yaatyanaavrittim anyayaa'vartate punah. 26. The bright and the dark paths of the world are verily thought to be eternal; by the one (the bright path) a person goes not to return again, and by the other (the dark path) he returns. COMMENTARY: The bright path is the path to the gods taken by devotees. The dark path is of the manes taken by those who perform sacrifices or charitable acts with the expectation of rewards. Naite sritee paartha jaanan yogee muhyati kashchana; Tasmaat sarveshu kaaleshu yogayukto bhavaarjuna. 27. Knowing these paths, O Arjuna, no Yogi is deluded! Therefore, at all times be steadfast in Yoga. Vedeshu yajneshu tapahsu chaiva Daaneshu yat punyaphalam pradishtam: 70 THE YOGA OF THE IMPERISHABLE BRAHMAN Atyeti tatsarvam idam viditwaa Yogee param sthaanamupaiti chaadyam. 28. Whatever fruits or merits is declared (in the scriptures) to accrue from (the study of) the Vedas, (the performance of) sacrifices, (the practice of) austerities, and (the offering of) gifts—beyond all these goes the Yogi, having known this; and he attains to the supreme primeval (first or ancient) Abode. Hari Om Tat Sat Iti Srimad Bhagavadgeetaasoopanishatsu Brahmavidyaayaam Yogashaastre Sri Krishnaarjunasamvaade Aksharabrahmayogo Naama Ashtamo'dhyaayah Thus in the Upanishads of the glorious Bhagavad Gita, the science of the Eternal, the scripture of Yoga, the dialogue between Sri Krishna and Arjuna, ends the eighth discourse entitled: "The Yoga Of the Imperishable Brahman"

CHAPTER THIRTEEN

THE KINGLY SCIENCE & THE KINGLY SECRET Summary of Ninth Discourse

Observing that Arjuna was a qualified aspirant and endowed with faith, Krishna declares to him the sovereign knowledge and sovereign secret that is to be known by direct experience. He adds that without faith in this knowledge man fails to reach God and is reborn to suffer. Now the Lord proceeds to describe His nature as the eternal, all-comprehensive Truth. He is everything that is invisible and visible. He pervades everything that exists. He creates everything, sustains everything, and when final dissolution takes place, absorbs everything into Himself. He manifests them again when the next creation begins. All beings who are ignorant of this knowledge are caught helplessly in the cycle of birth and death. In the midst of this creation, preservation and dissolution of the universe, the Lord stands as a silent witness, unaffected and unattached. He is the sole director, sustainer and supervisor of His Cosmic Prakriti. Ignorant beings are not able to recognise the Lord in one who has realised Him. Although these cruel beings assume a human form, their nature is that of demons. The God-realised Mahatma, on the other hand, is a man of knowledge, and perceives Him indwelling all beings and creatures. He beholds the underlying unity of existence in all names and forms. The Lord's divine protection is assured to all those who take refuge in Him. Whatever path a devotee follows, he ultimately reaches Him. He is the goal of the various methods of spiritual practice. Devotion, Sri Krishna emphasises, is the essence of all spiritual discipline. If this supreme 71 BHAGAVAD GITA element is present, then the devotee is freed from bondage. The Lord observes the motive and degree of devotion. Even the most sinful and diabolical man, if he takes a radical turn towards the path of righteousness and truth, reaches the Lord. Whatever vocation one follows, one can attain the Lord if one seeks earnestly and with loving devotion. The essential thing is to fix the mind on the Lord and dedicate everything unto Him—one's body, mind, actions, emotion and will. Sri Bhagavaan Uvaacha: Idam tu te guhyatamam pravakshyaamyanasooyave; Jnaanam vijnaanasahitam yajjnaatwaa mokshyase'shubhaat. The Blessed Lord said: 1. I shall now declare to thee who does not cavil, the greatest secret, the knowledge combined with experience (Self-realisation). Having known this, thou shalt be free from evil. Raajavidyaa raajaguhyam pavitramidamuttamam; Pratyakshaavagamam dharmyam susukham kartumavyayam. 2. This is the kingly science, the kingly secret, the supreme purifier, realisable by direct intuitional knowledge, according to righteousness, very easy to perform and imperishable. Ashraddhadhaanaah purushaa dharmasyaasya parantapa; Apraapya maam nivartante mrityusamsaaravartmani. 3. Those who have no faith in this Dharma (knowledge of the Self), O Parantapa (Arjuna), return to the path of this world of death without attaining Me! Mayaa tatamidam sarvam jagadavyaktamoortinaa; Matsthaani sarvabhootaani na chaaham teshvavasthitah. 4. All this world is pervaded by Me in My unmanifest aspect; all beings exist in Me, but I do not dwell in them. Na cha matsthaani bhootaani pashya me yogamaishwaram; Bhootabhrinna cha bhootastho mamaatmaa bhootabhaavanah. 5. Nor do beings exist in Me (in reality): behold My divine Yoga, supporting all beings, but not dwelling in them, is My Self, the efficient cause of beings. Yathaakaashasthito nityam vaayuh sarvatrago mahaan; Tathaa sarvaani bhootaani matsthaaneetyupadhaaraya. 6. As the mighty wind, moving everywhere, rests always in the ether, even so, know thou that all beings rest in Me. 72 THE YOGA OF THE KINGLY SCIENCE & THE KINGLY SECRET Sarvabhootaani kaunteya prakritim yaanti maamikaam; Kalpakshaye punastaani kalpaadau visrijaamyaham. 7. All beings, O Arjuna, enter into My Nature at the end of a Kalpa; I send them forth again at the beginning of (the next) Kalpa! Prakritim swaamavashtabhya visrijaami punah punah; Bhootagraamamimam kritsnamavasham prakritervashaat. 8. Animating My Nature, I again and again send forth all this multitude of beings, helpless by the force of Nature. Na cha maam taani karmaani nibadhnanti dhananjaya; Udaaseenavadaaseenam asaktam teshu karmasu. 9. These actions do not bind Me, O Arjuna, sitting like one indifferent, unattached to those acts!

Mayaa'dhyakshena prakritih sooyate sacharaacharam; Hetunaa'nena kaunteya jagadwiparivartate. 10. Under Me as supervisor, Nature produces the moving and the unmoving; because of this, O Arjuna, the world revolves! Avajaananti maam moodhaah maanusheem tanumaashritam; Param bhaavamajaananto mama bhootamaheshwaram. 11. Fools disregard Me, clad in human form, not knowing My higher Being as the great Lord of (all) beings. COMMENTARY: Fools who do not have discrimination despise Me, dwelling in human form. I have taken this body in order to bless My devotees. These fools have no knowledge of My higher Being. I am the great Lord, the Supreme. Moghaashaa moghakarmaano moghajnaanaa vichetasah; Raakshaseemaasureem chaiva prakritim mohineem shritaah. 12. Of vain hopes, of vain actions, of vain knowledge and senseless, they verily are possessed of the deceitful nature of demons and undivine beings. Mahaatmaanastu maam paartha daiveem prakritimaashritaah; Bhajantyananyamanaso jnaatwaa bhootaadimavyayam. 13. But the great souls, O Arjuna, partaking of My divine nature, worship Me with a single mind (with the mind devoted to nothing else), knowing Me as the imperishable source of beings! 73 BHAGAVAD GITA Satatam keertayanto maam yatantashcha dridhavrataah; Namasyantashcha maam bhaktyaa nityayuktaa upaasate. 14. Always glorifying Me, striving, firm in vows, prostrating before Me, they worship Me with devotion, ever steadfast. Jnaanayajnena chaapyanye yajanto maamupaasate; Ekatwena prithaktwena bahudhaa vishwatomukham. 15. Others also, sacrificing with the wisdom-sacrifice, worship Me, the all-faced, as one, as distinct, and as manifold. Aham kraturaham yajnah swadhaa'hamahamaushadham; Mantro'hamahamevaajyam ahamagniraham hutam. 16. I am the Kratu; I am the Yajna; I am the offering (food) to the manes; I am the medicinal herb and all the plants; I am the Mantra; I am also the ghee or melted butter; I am the fire; I am the oblation. Pitaahamasya jagato maataa dhaataa pitaamahah; Vedyam pavitramonkaara riksaama yajureva cha. 17. I am the father of this world, the mother, the dispenser of the fruits of actions, and the grandfather; the (one) thing to be known, the purifier, the sacred monosyllable (Om), and also the Rig-, the Sama- and Yajur Vedas. Gatirbhartaa prabhuh saakshee nivaasah sharanam suhrit; Prabhavah pralayah sthaanam nidhaanam beejamavyayam. 18. I am the goal, the support, the Lord, the witness, the abode, the shelter, the friend, the origin, the dissolution, the foundation, the treasure-house and the imperishable seed. Tapaamyahamaham varsham nigrihnaamyutsrijaami cha; Amritam chaiva mrityushcha sadasacchaahamarjuna. 19. (As the sun) I give heat; I withhold and send forth the rain; I am immortality and also death, existence and non-existence, O Arjuna! Traividyaa maam somapaah pootapaapaa Yajnairishtwaa swargatim praarthayante; Te punyamaasaadya surendralokaMashnanti divyaan divi devabhogaan. 20. The knowers of the three Vedas, the drinkers of Soma, purified of all sins, worshipping Me by sacrifices, pray for the way to heaven; they reach the holy world of the Lord of the gods and enjoy in heaven the divine pleasures of the gods. 74 THE YOGA OF THE KINGLY SCIENCE & THE KINGLY SECRET Te tam bhuktwaa swargalokam vishaalam Ksheene punye martyalokam vishanti; Evam trayeedharmamanuprapannaa Gataagatam kaamakaamaa labhante. 21. They, having enjoyed the vast heaven, enter the world of mortals when their merits are exhausted; thus abiding by the injunctions of the three (Vedas) and desiring (objects of) desires, they attain to the state of going and returning. COMMENTARY: When their accumulated merits are exhausted, they come to this world again. They have no independence. Ananyaashchintayanto maam ye janaah paryupaasate; Teshaam nityaabhiyuktaanaam yogakshemam vahaamyaham. 22. To those men who worship Me alone, thinking of no other, of those ever united, I secure what is not already possessed and preserve what they already possess. Ye'pyanyadevataa bhaktaa yajante shraddhayaa'nvitaah; Te'pi maameva kaunteya yajantyavidhipoorvakam. 23. Even those devotees who, endowed with faith, worship other gods, worship Me only, O Arjuna, but by the wrong method! Aham hi sarvayajnaanaam bhoktaa cha prabhureva cha; Na tu maamabhijaananti tattwenaatashchyavanti te. 24. (For) I alone am the enjoyer and also the Lord of all sacrifices; but they do not know Me in essence (in reality), and hence they fall (return to this mortal world). Yaanti devavrataa devaan pitreen yaanti pitrivrataah; Bhutaani yaanti bhutejyaa yaanti madyaajino'pi maam. 25. The worshippers of the gods go to them; to the manes go the ancestor-worshippers; to the Deities who preside over the elements go their worshippers; My devotees come to Me. Patram pushpam phalam toyam yo me bhaktyaa prayacchati; Tadaham bhaktyupahritamashnaami prayataatmanah. 26. Whoever offers Me with devotion and a pure mind (heart), a leaf, a flower, a fruit or a little water—I accept (this offering). Yatkaroshi yadashnaasi yajjuhoshi dadaasi yat; Yattapasyasi kaunteya tatkurushva madarpanam. 75 BHAGAVAD GITA 27. Whatever thou doest, whatever thou eatest, whatever thou offerest in sacrifice, whatever thou givest, whatever thou practiseth as austerity, O

Arjuna, do it as an offering unto Me! Shubhaashubhaphalairevam mokshyase karmabandhanaih; Sannyaasayogayuktaatmaa vimukto maamupaishyasi. 28. Thus shalt thou be freed from the bonds of actions yielding good and evil fruits; with the mind steadfast in the Yoga of renunciation, and liberated, thou shalt come unto Me. Samo'ham sarvabhooteshu na me dweshyo'sti na priyah; Ye bhajanti tu maam bhaktyaa mayi te teshu chaapyaham. 29. The same am I to all beings; to Me there is none hateful or dear; but those who worship Me with devotion are in Me and I am also in them. Api chet suduraachaaro bhajate maamananyabhaak; Saadhureva sa mantavyah samyagvyavasito hi sah. 30. Even if the most sinful worships Me, with devotion to none else, he too should indeed be regarded as righteous, for he has rightly resolved. Kshipram bhavati dharmaatmaa shashwacchaantim nigacchati; Kaunteya pratijaaneehi na me bhaktah pranashyati. 31. Soon he becomes righteous and attains to eternal peace; O Arjuna, know thou for certain that My devotee is never destroyed! Maam hi paartha vyapaashritya ye'pi syuh paapayonayah; Striyo vaishyaastathaa shoodraaste'pi yaanti paraam gatim. 32. For, taking refuge in Me, they also, who, O Arjuna, may be of sinful birth—women, Vaisyas as well as Sudras—attain the Supreme Goal! Kim punarbraahmanaah punyaa bhaktaa raajarshayastathaa; Anityamasukham lokam imam praapya bhajaswa maam. 33. How much more easily then the holy Brahmins and devoted royal saints (attain the goal); having obtained this impermanent and unhappy world, do thou worship Me. Manmanaa bhava madbhakto madyaajee maam namaskuru; Maamevaishyasi yuktwaivamaatmaanam matparaayanah. 34. Fix thy mind on Me; be devoted to Me; sacrifice unto Me; bow down to Me; having thus united thy whole self with Me, taking Me as the Supreme Goal, thou shalt verily come unto Me. 76 THE YOGA OF THE KINGLY SCIENCE & THE KINGLY SECRET COMMENTARY: The whole being of a man should be surrendered to the Lord without reservation. Then there will be a marvellous transformation. He will have the vision of God everywhere. All sorrows and pains will vanish. His mind will be one with Him. He will for ever have his life and being in the Lord alone.

CHAPTER FOURTEEN

THE DIVINE GLORIES
Summary of Tenth Discourse

Krishna tells Arjuna that even the Devas and highly evolved souls fail to understand how He projects Himself as the universe and all its manifestations. He goes on to describe the various qualities that beings manifest according to their Karmas. All these qualities—wisdom, truth, contentment, etc.—originate from Him. The true devotees of the Lord are wholly absorbed in Him. They have completely surrendered to Him and through single-minded devotion they are granted the power of discrimination, the discrimination that leads them from the unreal to the Real. Krishna emphatically declares that ignorance is destroyed and knowledge gained through Divine Grace alone. Arjuna accepts the descent of the Supreme in a human form, but wishes to know from the Lord Himself His Cosmic powers by means of which He controls the diverse forces of the universe. The Lord describes His Divine glories, bringing within the range of Arjuna's comprehension His limitless manifestations, and how He upholds everything. In short, the Lord is the Almighty Power that creates, sustains and destroys everything. Sri Bhagavaan Uvaacha: Bhooya eva mahaabaaho shrinu me paramam vachah; Yatte'ham preeyamaanaaya vakshyaami hitakaamyayaa. The Blessed Lord said: 77 BHAGAVAD GITA 1. Again, O mighty-armed Arjuna, listen to My supreme word which I shall declare to thee who art beloved, for thy welfare! COMMENTARY: The all-compassionate Lord in His mercy wants to encourage Arjuna and cheer him up, and so He Himself comes forward to give him instructions without any request having been made by Arjuna. Na me viduh suraganaah prabhavam na maharshayah; Ahamaadirhi devaanaam maharsheenaam cha sarvashah. 2. Neither the hosts of the gods nor the great sages know My origin; for, in every way I am the source of all the gods and the great sages. Yo maamajamanaadim cha vetti lokamaheshwaram; Asammoodhah sa martyeshu sarvapaapaih pramuchyate. 3. He who knows Me as unborn and beginningless, as the great Lord of the worlds, he, among mortals, is undeluded; he is liberated from all sins. COMMENTARY: As the Supreme Being is the cause of all the worlds, He is beginningless. As He is the source of all the gods and the great sages, so there is no source for His own existence. As He is beginningless, He is unborn. He is the great Lord of all the worlds. Buddhir jnaanamasammohah kshamaa satyam damah shamah; Sukham duhkham bhavo'bhaavo bhayam chaabhayameva cha. 4. Intellect, wisdom, non-delusion, forgiveness, truth, self-restraint, calmness, happiness, pain, birth or existence, death or non-existence, fear and also fearlessness, Ahimsaa samataa tushtistapo daanam yasho'yashah; Bhavanti bhaavaa bhootaanaam matta eva prithagvidhaah. 5. Non-injury, equanimity, contentment, austerity, fame, beneficence, ill-fame—(these) different kinds of qualities of beings arise from Me alone. Maharshayah sapta poorve chatwaaro manavastathaa; Madbhaavaa maanasaa jaataa yeshaam loka imaah prajaah. 6. The seven great sages, the ancient four and also the Manus, possessed of powers like Me (on account of their minds being fixed on Me), were born of (My) mind; from them are these creatures born in this world. Etaam vibhootim yogam cha mama yo vetti tattwatah; So'vikampena yogena yujyate naatra samshayah. 78 THE YOGA OF THE DIVINE GLORIES 7. He who in truth knows these manifold manifestations of My Being and (this) Yoga-power of Mine, becomes established in the unshakeable Yoga; there is no doubt about it. Aham sarvasya prabhavo mattah sarvam pravartate; Iti matwaa bhajante maam budhaa bhaavasamanvitaah. 8. I am the source of all; from Me everything evolves; understanding thus, the wise, endowed with meditation, worship Me. Macchittaa madgatapraanaa bodhayantah parasparam; Kathayantashcha maam nityam tushyanti cha ramanti cha. 9. With their minds and lives entirely absorbed in Me, enlightening each other and always speaking of Me, they are satisfied and delighted. Teshaam satatayuktaanaam bhajataam preetipoorvakam; Dadaami buddhiyogam tam yena maamupayaanti te. 10. To them who are ever steadfast, worshipping Me with love, I give the Yoga of discrimination by which they come to Me. COMMENTARY: The devotees who have dedicated themselves to the Lord, who are ever harmonious and self-abiding, who adore Him with intense love, who are ever devout, obtain the Divine Grace. Teshaam evaanukampaartham aham ajnaanajam tamah; Naashayaamyaatmabhaavastho jnaanadeepena bhaaswataa. 11. Out of mere compassion for them, I, dwelling within their Self, destroy the darkness born of ignorance by the luminous lamp of knowledge. Arjuna Uvaacha: Param brahma param dhaama pavitram paramam bhavaan; Purusham shaashvatam divyam aadidevamajam vibhum. Arjuna said: 12. Thou art the Supreme Brahman, the supreme abode (or the supreme light), the supreme purifier, the eternal, divine Person, the primeval God, unborn and omnipresent. Aahustwaam rishayah sarve devarshirnaaradastathaa; Asito devalo vyaasah swayam chaiva braveeshi me. 13. All the sages have thus declared Thee, as also the divine sage Narada; so also Asita, Devala and Vyasa; and now Thou Thyself sayest so to me. 79 BHAGAVAD GITA Sarvametadritam manye yanmaam vadasi keshava; Na hi te bhagavan vyaktim vidurdevaa na daanavaah. 14. I believe all this that Thou sayest to me as true, O Krishna! Verily, O blessed Lord, neither the gods nor the demons know Thy manifestation (origin)! Swayamevaatmanaatmaanam vettha twam purushottama; Bhootabhaavana bhootesha devadeva jagatpate. 15. Verily, Thou Thyself knowest Thyself by Thyself, O Supreme Person, O source and Lord of beings, O God of gods, O ruler of the world! Vaktum arhasyasheshena divyaa hyaatmavibhootayah; Yaabhir vibhootibhir lokaanimaamstwam vyaapya tishthasi. 16. Thou shouldst indeed tell, without reserve, of Thy divine glories by which Thou existeth, pervading all these worlds. (None else can do so.) Katham vidyaamaham yogimstwaam sadaa parichintayan; Keshu keshu cha bhaaveshu chintyo'si bhagavanmayaa. 17. How shall I, ever meditating, know Thee, O Yogin? In what aspects or things, O blessed Lord, art Thou to be thought of by me? Vistarenaatmano yogam vibhootim cha janaardana; Bhooyah kathaya triptirhi shrinvato naasti me'mritam. 18. Tell me again in detail, O Krishna, of Thy Yogic power and glory; for I am not satisfied with what I have heard of Thy life-giving and nectar-like speech! Sri Bhagavaan Uvaacha: Hanta te kathayishyaami divyaa hyaatmavibhootayah; Praadhaanyatah kurushreshtha naastyanto vistarasya me. The Blessed Lord said: 19. Very well, now I will declare to thee My divine glories in their prominence, O Arjuna! There is no end to their detailed description. COMMENTARY: The Lord's divine glories are illimitable. Ahamaatmaa gudaakesha sarvabhootaashayasthitah; Ahamaadishcha madhyam cha bhootaanaamanta eva cha. 20. I am the Self, O Gudakesha, seated in the hearts of all beings! I am the beginning, the middle and also the end of all beings. 80 THE YOGA OF THE DIVINE GLORIES Aadityaanaamaham vishnur jyotishaam raviramshumaan; Mareechirmarutaamasmi nakshatraanaamaham shashee. 21. Among the (twelve) Adityas, I am Vishnu; among the luminaries, the radiant sun; I am Marichi among the (seven or forty-nine) Maruts; among stars the moon am I. Vedaanaam saamavedo'smi devaanaam asmi vaasavah; Indriyaanaam manashchaasmi bhootaanaamasmi chetanaa. 22. Among the VedasI am the Sama Veda; I am Vasava among the gods; among the senses I am the mind; and I am intelligence among living beings. Rudraanaam shankarashchaasmi vittesho yaksharakshasaam; Vasoonaam paavakashchaasmi meruh shikharinaamaham. 23. And, among the Rudras I am Shankara; among the Yakshas and Rakshasas, the Lord of wealth (Kubera); among the Vasus I am Pavaka (fire); and among the (seven) mountains I am the Meru. Purodhasaam cha mukhyam maam viddhipaartha brihaspatim; Senaaneenaamaham skandah sarasaamasmi saagarah. 24. And, among the household priests (of kings), O Arjuna, know Me to be the chief, Brihaspati; among the army generals I am Skanda; among lakes I am the ocean! Maharsheenaam bhriguraham giraamasmyekamaksharam; Yajnaanaam japayajno'smi sthaavaraanaam himaalayah. 25. Among the great sages I am Bhrigu; among words I am the monosyllable Om; among sacrifices I am the sacrifice of silent repetition; among immovable things the Himalayas I am. COMMENTARY: Repetition of the Mantra is regarded as the best of all Yajnas or sacrifices. There is no loss or injury in this Yajna. Manu says: "Whatever else the Brahmana may or may not do, he attains salvation by Japa alone". Ashwatthah sarvavrikshaanaam devarsheenaam cha naaradah; Gandharvaanaam chitrarathah siddhaanaam kapilo munih. 26. Among the trees (I am) the peepul; among the divine sages I am Narada; among Gandharvas I am Chitraratha; among the perfected the sage Kapila. Ucchaihshravasamashwaanaam viddhi maamamritodbhavam; Airaavatam gajendraanaam naraanaam cha naraadhipam. 27. Know Me as Ucchaisravas, born of nectar among horses; among lordly elephants (I am) the Airavata; and among men, the king. 81 BHAGAVAD GITA Aayudhaanaamaham vajram dhenoonaamasmi kaamadhuk; Prajanashchaasmi kandarpah sarpaanaamasmi vaasukih. 28. Among weapons I am the thunderbolt; among cows I am the wish-fulfilling cow called Surabhi; I am the progenitor, the god of love; among serpents I am Vasuki. Anantashchaasmi naagaanaam varuno yaadasaamaham; Pitreenaamaryamaa chaasmi yamah samyamataamaham. 29. I am Ananta among the Nagas; I am Varuna among water-Deities; Aryaman among the manes I am; I am Yama among the governors. Prahlaadashchaasmi daityaanaam kaalah kalayataamaham; Mrigaanaam cha mrigendro'ham vainateyashcha pakshinaam. 30. And, I am

Prahlad among the demons; among the reckoners I am time; among beasts I am their king, the lion; and Garuda among birds. Pavanah pavataamasmi raamah shastrabhritaamaham; Jhashaanaam makarashchaasmi srotasaamasmi jaahnavee. 31. Among the purifiers (or the speeders) I am the wind; Rama among the warriors am I; among the fishes I am the shark; among the streams I am the Ganga. Sargaanaamaadirantashcha madhyam chaivaaham arjuna; Adhyaatmavidyaa vidyaanaam vaadah pravadataamaham. 32. Among creations I am the beginning, the middle and also the end, O Arjuna! Among the sciences I am the science of the Self; and I am logic among controversialists. Aksharaanaamakaaro'smi dwandwah saamaasikasya cha; Ahamevaakshayah kaalo dhaataaham vishwatomukhah. 33. Among the letters of the alphabet, the letter "A" I am, and the dual among the compounds. I am verily the inexhaustible or everlasting time; I am the dispenser (of the fruits of actions), having faces in all directions. Mrityuh sarvaharashchaaham udbhavashcha bhavishyataam; Keertih shreervaakcha naareenaam smritirmedhaadhritih kshamaa. 34. And I am all-devouring death, and prosperity of those who are to be prosperous; among feminine qualities (I am) fame, prosperity, speech, memory, intelligence, firmness and forgiveness. Brihatsaama tathaa saamnaam gaayatree cchandasaamaham; Maasaanaam maargasheersho'hamritoonaam kusumaakarah. 82 THE YOGA OF THE DIVINE GLORIES 35. Among the hymns also I am the Brihatsaman; among metres Gayatri am I; among the months I am Margasirsa; among seasons (I am) the flowery season. Dyootam cchalayataamasmi tejastejaswinaamaham; Jayo'smi vyavasaayo'smi sattwam sattwavataamaham. 36. I am the gambling of the fraudulent; I am the splendour of the splendid; I am victory; I am determination (of those who are determined); I am the goodness of the good. COMMENTARY: Of the various methods of defrauding others, I am gambling, such as dice-play. Gambling is My manifestation. I am power in the powerful. I am victory in the victorious. I am effort in those who make that effort. Vrishneenaam vaasudevo'smi paandavaanaam dhananjayah; Muneenaamapyaham vyaasah kaveenaamushanaa kavih. 37. Among Vrishnis I am Vasudeva; among the Pandavas I am Arjuna; among sages I am Vyasa; among poets I am Usana, the poet. Dando damayataamasmi neetirasmi jigeeshataam; Maunam chaivaasmi guhyaanaam jnaanam jnaanavataamaham. 38. Among the punishers I am the sceptre; among those who seek victory I am statesmanship; and also among secrets I am silence; knowledge among knowers I am. Yachchaapi sarvabhootaanaam beejam tadahamarjuna; Na tadasti vinaa yatsyaanmayaa bhootam charaacharam. 39. And whatever is the seed of all beings, that also am I, O Arjuna! There is no being, whether moving or unmoving, that can exist without Me. COMMENTARY: I am the primeval seed from which all creation has come into existence. I am the seed of everything. I am the Self of everything. Nothing can exist without Me. Everything is of My nature. I am the soul of everything. Naanto'sti mama divyaanaam vibhooteenaam parantapa; Esha tooddeshatah prokto vibhootervistaro mayaa. 40. There is no end to My divine glories, O Arjuna, but this is a brief statement by Me of the particulars of My divine glories! Yadyad vibhootimat sattwam shreemadoorjitameva vaa; Tattadevaavagaccha twam mama tejom'shasambhavam. 41. Whatever being there is that is glorious, prosperous or powerful, that know thou to be a manifestation of a part of My splendour. 83 BHAGAVAD GITA Athavaa bahunaitena kim jnaatena tavaarjuna; Vishtabhyaahamidam kritsnamekaamshena sthito jagat. 42. But of what avail to thee is the knowledge of all these details, O Arjuna? I exist, supporting this whole world by one part of Myself.

CHAPTER FIFTEEN

THE VISION OF THE COSMIC FORM Summary of Eleventh Discourse

Arjuna's doubts having been removed through a clear description of the nature of the Atman and the origin and destruction of all created things, he is now ready to behold the Cosmic Vision. Krishna grants him the divine sight by means of which Arjuna beholds the Lord as the vast Cosmic Manifestation. The vision is at once all-comprehensive and simultaneous. In every direction Arjuna sees the Lord as the entire universe. All the created worlds, gods, beings, creatures and things stand revealed as the one gigantic body of the Lord. Arjuna further sees that the great cosmic drama is set in motion and controlled by the all-mighty power of the Lord. His Will alone prevails in all things and actions, both good and bad. The Lord exhorts him to fight, he being only an apparent cause of the destruction of his enemies. Arjuna is unable to bear the pressure of the sudden expansion of consciousness and is filled with fear. He begs the Lord to assume once more His usual form. Krishna reiterates that this vision cannot be had through any amount of austerities, study, sacrifices or philanthrophic acts. Supreme devotion is the only means by which one can have access to His grand vision. Arjuna Uvaacha: Madanugrahaaya paramam guhyamadhyaatmasamjnitam; Yattwayoktam vachastena moho'yam vigato mama. 84 THE YOGA OF THE DIVINE GLORIES Arjuna said: 1. By this explanation of the highest secret concerning the Self, which Thou hast spoken out of compassion towards me my delusion is gone. COMMENTARY: After hearing the glories of the Lord, Arjuna has an intense longing to have the wonderful Cosmic Vision. Bhavaapyayau hi bhootaanaam shrutau vistarasho mayaa; Twattah kamalapatraaksha maahaatmyamapi chaavyayam. 2. The origin and the destruction of beings verily have been heard by me in detail from Thee, O lotus-eyed Lord, and also Thy inexhaustible greatness! Evametadyathaattha twamaatmaanam parameshwara; Drashtumicchaami te roopamaishwaram purushottama. 3. (Now), O Supreme Lord, as Thou hast thus described Thyself, O Supreme Person, I wish to see Thy Divine Form! Manyase yadi tacchakyam mayaa drashtumiti prabho; Yogeshwara tato me twam darshayaatmaanamavyayam. 4. If Thou, O Lord, thinkest it possible for me to see it, do Thou, then, O Lord of the Yogis, show me Thy imperishable Self! Sri Bhagavaan Uvaacha: Pashya me paartha roopaani shatasho'tha sahasrashah; Naanaavidhaani divyaani naanaavarnaakriteeni cha. The Blessed Lord said: 5. Behold, O Arjuna, My forms by the hundreds and thousands, of different sorts, divine and of various colours and shapes! Pashyaadityaan vasoon rudraan ashwinau marutastathaa; Bahoonyadrishtapoorvaani pashyaashcharyaani bhaarata. 6. Behold the Adityas, the Vasus, the Rudras, the two Asvins and also the Maruts; behold many wonders never seen before, O Arjuna! Ihaikastham jagatkritsnam pashyaadya sacharaacharam; Mama dehe gudaakesha yachchaanyad drashtumicchasi. 7. Now behold, O Arjuna, in this, My body, the whole universe centred in the one—including the moving and the unmoving—and whatever else thou desirest to see! 85 BHAGAVAD GITA Na tu maam shakyase drashtum anenaiva swachakshushaa; Divyam dadaami te chakshuh pashya me yogamaishwaram. 8. But thou art not able to behold Me with these, thine own eyes; I give thee the divine eye; behold My lordly Yoga. COMMENTARY: No fleshy eye can behold Me in My Cosmic Form. One can see Me only through the eye of intuition or the divine eye. It should not be confused with seeing through the physical eye or through the mind. It is an inner divine experience attained through intense devotion and concentration. Sanjaya Uvaacha: Evamuktwaa tato raajan mahaayogeshwaro harih; Darshayaamaasa paarthaaya paramam roopamaishwaram. Sanjaya said: 9. Having thus spoken, O king, the great Lord of Yoga, Hari (Krishna), showed to Arjuna His supreme form as the Lord! Anekavaktra nayanam anekaadbhuta darshanam; Anekadivyaabharanam divyaanekodyataayudham. 10. With numerous mouths and eyes, with numerous wonderful sights, with numerous divine ornaments, with numerous divine weapons uplifted (such a form He showed). Divyamaalyaambaradharam divyagandhaanulepanam; Sarvaashcharyamayam devam anantam vishwatomukham. 11. Wearing divine garlands and apparel, anointed with divine unguents, the all-wonderful, resplendent (Being), endless, with faces on all sides, Divi sooryasahasrasya bhavedyugapadutthitaa; Yadi bhaah sadrishee saa syaadbhaasastasya mahaatmanah. 12. If the splendour of a thousand suns were to blaze out at once (simultaneously) in the sky, that would be the splendour of that mighty Being (great soul). Tatraikastham jagatkritsnam pravibhaktamanekadhaa; Apashyaddevadevasya shareere paandavastadaa. 13. There, in the body of the God of gods, Arjuna then saw the whole universe resting in the one, with its many groups. Tatah sa vismayaavishto hrishtaromaa dhananjayah; Pranamya shirasaa devam kritaanjalirabhaashata. 86 THE YOGA OF THE VISION OF THE COSMIC FORM 14. Then, Arjuna, filled with wonder and with hair standing on end, bowed down his head to the Lord and spoke with joined palms. Arjuna Uvaacha: Pashyaami devaamstava deva dehe Sarvaamstathaa bhootavisheshasanghaan; Brahmaanameesham kamalaasanasthaMrisheemshcha sarvaanuragaamshcha divyaan. Arjuna said: 15. I behold all the gods, O God, in Thy body, and hosts of various classes of beings; Brahma, the Lord, seated on the lotus, all the sages and the celestial serpents! Anekabaahoodaravaktranetram Pashyaami twaam sarvato'nantaroopam; Naantam na madhyam na punastavaadim Pashyaami vishweshwara vishwaroopa. 16. I see Thee of boundless form on every side, with many arms, stomachs, mouths and eyes; neither the end nor the middle nor also the beginning do I see, O Lord of the universe, O Cosmic Form! Kireetinam gadinam chakrinam cha, Tejoraashim sarvato deeptimantam; Pashyaami twaam durnireekshyam samantaad Deeptaanalaarkadyutimaprameyam. 17. I see Thee with the diadem, the club and the discus, a mass of radiance shining everywhere, very hard to look at, blazing all round like burning fire and the sun, and immeasurable. Twamaksharam paramam veditavyam Twamasya vishwasya param nidhaanam; Twamavyayah shaashwatadharmagoptaa Sanaatanastwam purusho mato me. 18. Thou art the Imperishable, the Supreme Being, worthy of being known; Thou art the great treasure-house of this universe; Thou art the imperishable protector of the eternal Dharma; Thou art the ancient Person, I deem. Anaadimadhyaantamanantaveeryam Anantabaahum shashisooryanetram; Pashyaami twaam deeptahutaashavaktram Swatejasaa vishwamidam tapantam. 87 BHAGAVAD GITA 19. I see Thee without beginning, middle or end, infinite in power, of endless arms, the sun and the moon being Thy eyes, the burning fire Thy mouth, heating the entire universe with Thy radiance. Dyaavaaprithivyoridamantaram hi Vyaaptam twayaikena dishashcha sarvaah; Drishtwaa'dbhutam roopamugram tavedam Lokatrayam pravyathitam mahaatman. 20. The space between the earth and the heaven and all the quarters are filled by Thee alone; having seen this, Thy wonderful and terrible form, the three worlds are trembling with fear, O great-souled Being! Amee hi twaam surasanghaah vishanti Kechid bheetaah praanjalayo grinanti; Swasteetyuktwaa maharshisiddhasanghaah Stuvanti twaam stutibhih pushkalaabhih. 21. Verily, into Thee enter these hosts of gods; some extol Thee in fear with joined palms: "May it be well." Saying thus, bands of great sages and perfected ones praise Thee with complete hymns. Rudraadityaa vasavo ye cha saadhyaa Vishwe'shvinau marutashchoshmapaashcha; Gandharvayakshaasurasiddhasanghaa Veekshante twaam vismitaashchaiva sarve. 22. The Rudras, Adityas, Vasus, Sadhyas, Visvedevas, the two Asvins, Maruts, the manes and hosts of celestial singers, Yakshas, demons and the perfected ones, are all looking at Thee in great astonishment. Roopam mahat te bahuvaktranetram Mahaabaaho bahubaahoorupaadam; Bahoodaram bahudamshtraakaraalam Drishtwaa lokaah pravyathitaastathaa'ham. 23. Having beheld Thy immeasurable form with many mouths and eyes, O mighty-armed, with many arms, thighs and feet, with many stomachs, and fearful with many teeth, the worlds are terrified and so am I! Nabhahsprisham deeptamanekavarnam Vyaattaananam deeptavishaalanetram; Drishtwaa hi twaam pravyathitaantaraatmaa Dhritim na vindaami shamam cha vishno. 88 THE YOGA OF THE VISION OF THE COSMIC FORM 24. On seeing Thee (the Cosmic Form) touching the sky, shining in many colours, with mouths wide open, with large, fiery eyes, I am terrified at heart and find neither courage nor peace, O Vishnu! Damshtraakaraalaani cha te mukhaani Drishtwaiva kaalaanalasannibhaani; Disho na jaane na labhe cha sharma Praseeda devesha jagannivaasa. 25. Having seen Thy mouths, fearful with teeth, blazing like the fires of cosmic dissolution, I know not the four quarters, nor do I find peace. Have mercy, O Lord of the gods! O abode of the universe! Amee cha twaam dhritaraashtrasya putraah Sarve sahaivaavanipaalasanghaih; Bheeshmo dronah sootaputrastathaa'sau Sahaasmadeeyairapi yodhamukhyaih. 26. All the sons of Dhritarashtra with the hosts of kings of the earth, Bhishma, Drona and Karna, with the chief among all our warriors, Vaktraani te twaramaanaa vishanti Damshtraakaraalaani bhayaanakaani; Kechidwilagnaa dashanaantareshu

Sandrishyante choornitairuttamaangaih. 27. They hurriedly enter into Thy mouths with terrible teeth and fearful to behold. Some are found sticking in the gaps between the teeth, with their heads crushed to powder. Yathaa nadeenaam bahavo'mbuvegaah Samudramevaabhimukhaah dravanti; Tathaa tavaamee naralokaveeraah Vishanti vaktraanyabhivijwalanti. 28. Verily, just as many torrents of rivers flow towards the ocean, even so these heroes of the world of men enter Thy flaming mouths. COMMENTARY: Arjuna sees all the warriors, whom he did not wish to kill, rushing to death. He knows now that the Lord has already destroyed them, so why should he worry about the inevitable. Yathaa pradeeptam jwalanam patangaa Vishanti naashaaya samriddhavegaah; Tathaiva naashaaya vishanti lokaas Tavaapi vaktraani samriddhavegaah. 89 BHAGAVAD GITA 29. As moths hurriedly rush into a blazing fire for (their own) destruction, so also these creatures hurriedly rush into Thy mouths for (their own) destruction. Lelihyase grasamaanah samantaal Lokaan samagraan vadanair jwaladbhih; Tejobhiraapoorya jagatsamagram Bhaasastavograah pratapanti vishno. 30. Thou lickest up, devouring all the worlds on every side with Thy flaming mouths. Thy fierce rays, filling the whole world with radiance, are burning, O Vishnu! Aakhyaahi me ko bhavaanugraroopo Namo'stu te devavara praseeda; Vijnaatumicchaami bhavantamaadyam Na hi prajaanaami tava pravrittim. 31. Tell me, who Thou art, so fierce in form. Salutations to Thee, O God Supreme! Have mercy; I desire to know Thee, the original Being. I know not indeed Thy doing. Sri Bhagavaan Uvaacha: Kaalo'smi lokakshayakrit pravriddho Lokaan samaahartumiha pravrittah; Rite'pi twaam na bhavishyanti sarve Ye'wasthitaah pratyaneekeshu yodhaah. The Blessed Lord said: 32. I am the mighty world-destroying Time, now engaged in destroying the worlds. Even without thee, none of the warriors arrayed in the hostile armies shall live. Tasmaat twam uttishtha yasho labhaswa Jitwaa shatroon bhungkshwa raajyam samriddham; Mayaivaite nihataah poorvameva Nimittamaatram bhava savyasaachin. 33. Therefore, stand up and obtain fame. Conquer the enemies and enjoy the unrivalled kingdom. Verily, they have already been slain by Me; be thou a mere instrument, O Arjuna! Dronam cha bheeshmam cha jayadratham cha Karnam tathaa'nyaanapi yodhaveeraan; Mayaa hataamstwam jahi maa vyathishthaa Yudhyaswa jetaasi rane sapatnaan. 34. Drona, Bhishma, Jayadratha, Karna and all the other courageous warriors—these have already been slain by Me; do thou kill; be not distressed with fear; fight and thou shalt conquer thy enemies in battle. 90 THE YOGA OF THE VISION OF THE COSMIC

FORM Sanjaya Uvaacha: Etacchrutwaa vachanam keshavasya Kritaanjalirvepamaanah kireetee; Namaskritwaa bhooya evaaha krishnam Sagadgadam bheetabheetah pranamya. Sanjaya said: 35. Having heard that speech of Lord Krishna, the crowned one (Arjuna), with joined palms, trembling, prostrating himself, again addressed Krishna, in a choked voice, bowing down, overwhelmed with fear. Arjuna Uvaacha: Sthaane hrisheekesha tava prakeertyaa Jagat prahrishyatyanurajyate cha; Rakshaamsi bheetaani disho dravanti Sarve namasyanti cha siddhasanghaah. Arjuna said: 36. It is meet, O Krishna, that the world delights and rejoices in Thy praise; demons fly in fear to all quarters and the hosts of the perfected ones bow to Thee! Kasmaachcha te na nameran mahaatman Gareeyase brahmano'pyaadikartre; Ananta devesha jagannivaasa Twamaksharam sadasattatparam yat. 37. And why should they not, O great soul, bow to Thee who art greater (than all else), the primal cause even of (Brahma) the creator, O Infinite Being! O Lord of the gods! O abode of the universe! Thou art the imperishable, the Being, the non-being and That which is the supreme (that which is beyond the Being and non-being). COMMENTARY: The Lord is Mahatma. He is greater than all else. He is the imperishable, so He is the proper object of worship, love and delight. Twamaadidevah purushah puraanas Twamasya vishwasya param nidhaanam; Vettaasi vedyam cha param cha dhaama Twayaa tatam vishwamanantaroopa. 38. Thou art the primal God, the ancient Purusha, the supreme refuge of this universe, the knower, the knowable and the supreme abode. By Thee is the universe pervaded, O Being of infinite forms! Vaayuryamo'gnirvarunah shashaankah 91 BHAGAVAD GITA Prajaapatistwam prapitaamahashcha; Namo namaste'stu sahasrakritwah Punashcha bhooyo'pi namo namaste. 39. Thou art Vayu, Yama, Agni, Varuna, the moon, the creator, and the great-grandfather. Salutations, salutations unto Thee, a thousand times, and again salutations, salutations unto Thee! Namah purastaadatha prishthataste Namo'stu te sarvata eva sarva; Anantaveeryaamitavikramastwam Sarvam samaapnoshi tato'si sarvah. 40. Salutations to Thee from front and from behind! Salutations to Thee on every side! O All! Thou infinite in power and prowess, pervadest all; wherefore Thou art all. Sakheti matwaa prasabham yaduktam He krishna he yaadava he sakheti; Ajaanataa mahimaanam tavedam Mayaa pramaadaat pranayena vaapi. 41. Whatever I have presumptuously uttered from love or carelessness, addressing Thee as O Krishna! O Yadava! O Friend! regarding Thee merely as a friend, unknowing of this, Thy greatness, Yachchaavahaasaartham asatkrito'si Vihaarashayyaasanabhojaneshu; Eko'thavaapyachyuta tatsamaksham Tatkshaamaye twaamaham aprameyam. 42. In whatever way I may have insulted Thee for the sake of fun while at play, reposing, sitting or at meals, when alone (with Thee), O Achyuta, or in company—that I implore Thee, immeasurable one, to forgive! Pitaasi lokasya charaacharasya Twamasya poojyashcha gururgareeyaan; Na twatsamo'styabhyadhikah kuto'nyo Lokatraye'pyapratimaprabhaava. 43. Thou art the Father of this world, unmoving and moving. Thou art to be adored by this world. Thou art the greatest Guru; (for) none there exists who is equal to Thee; how then can there be another superior to Thee in the three worlds, O Being of unequalled power? Tasmaatpranamya pranidhaaya kaayam Prasaadaye twaamahameeshameedyam; Piteva putrasya sakheva sakhyuh Priyah priyaayaarhasi deva sodhum. 92 THE YOGA OF THE VISION OF THE COSMIC FORM 44. Therefore, bowing down, prostrating my body, I crave Thy forgiveness, O adorable Lord! As a father forgives his son, a friend his (dear) friend, a lover his beloved, even so shouldst Thou forgive me, O God! Adrishtapoorvam hrishito'smi drishtwaa Bhayena cha pravyathitam mano me; Tadeva me darshaya deva roopam Praseeda devesha jagannivaasa. 45. I am delighted, having seen what has never been seen before; and yet my mind is distressed with fear. Show me that (previous) form only, O God! Have mercy, O God of gods! O abode of the universe! Kireetinam gadinam chakrahastam Icchaami twaam drashtumaham tathaiva; Tenaiva roopena chaturbhujena Sahasrabaaho bhava vishwamoorte. 46. I desire to see Thee as before, crowned, bearing a mace, with the discus in hand, in Thy former form only, having four arms, O thousand-armed, Cosmic Form (Being)! Sri Bhagavaan Uvaacha: Mayaa prasannena tavaarjunedam Roopam param darshitamaatmayogaat; Tejomayam vishwamanantamaadyam Yanme twadanyena na drishtapoorvam. The Blessed Lord said: 47. O Arjuna, this Cosmic Form has graciously been shown to thee by Me by My own Yogic power; full of splendour, primeval, and infinite, this Cosmic Form of Mine has never been seen before by anyone other than thyself. Na vedayajnaadhyayanairna daanair Na cha kriyaabhirna tapobhirugraih; Evam roopah shakya aham nriloke Drashtum twadanyena karupraveera. 48. Neither by the study of the Vedas and sacrifices, nor by gifts, nor by rituals, nor by severe austerities, can I be seen in this form in the world of men by any other than thyself, O great hero of the Kurus (Arjuna)! Maa te vyathaa maa cha vimoodhabhaavo Drishtwaa roopam ghorameedringmamedam;

Vyapetabheeh preetamanaah punastwam Tadeva me roopamidam prapashya. 93 BHAGAVAD GITA 49. Be not afraid nor bewildered on seeing such a terrible form of Mine as this; with thy fear entirely dispelled and with a gladdened heart, now behold again this former form of Mine. Sanjaya Uvaacha: Ityarjunam vaasudevastathoktwaa Swakam roopam darshayaamaasa bhooyah; Aashwaasayaamaasa cha bheetamenam Bhootwaa punah saumyavapurmahaatmaa. Sanjaya said: 50. Having thus spoken to Arjuna, Krishna again showed His own form; and the great soul (Krishna), assuming His gentle form, consoled him who was terrified (Arjuna). Arjuna Uvaacha: Drishtwedam maanusham roopam tava saumyam janaardana; Idaaneemasmi samvrittah sachetaah prakritim gatah. Arjuna said: 51. Having seen this Thy gentle human form, O Krishna, now I am composed and restored to my own nature! Sri Bhagavaan Uvaacha: Sudurdarshamidam roopam drishtavaanasi yanmama; Devaa apyasya roopasya nityam darshanakaangkshinah. The Blessed Lord said: 52. Very hard indeed it is to see this form of Mine which thou hast seen. Even the gods are ever longing to behold it. Naa ham vedairna tapasaa na daanena na chejyayaa; Shakya evamvidho drashtum drishtavaanasi maam yathaa. 53. Neither by the Vedas, nor by austerity, nor by gift, nor by sacrifice, can I be seen in this form as thou hast seen Me (so easily). Bhaktyaa twananyayaa shakyam aham evamvidho'rjuna; Jnaatum drashtum cha tattwena praveshtum cha parantapa. 54. But by single-minded devotion can I, of this form, be known and seen in reality and also entered into, O Arjuna! Matkarmakrinmatparamo madbhaktah sangavarjitah; Nirvairah sarvabhooteshu yah sa maameti paandava. 94 THE YOGA OF THE VISION OF THE COSMIC FORM 55. He who does all actions for Me, who looks upon Me as the Supreme, who is devoted to Me, who is free from attachment, who bears enmity towards no creature, he comes to Me, O Arjuna! COMMENTARY: This is the essence of the whole teaching of the Gita. He who practises this teaching attains supreme bliss and immortality. Such a one realises Him and enters into His Being, becoming completely one with Him. This verse contains the summary of the entire Gita philosophy.

CHAPTER SIXTEEN

DEVOTION Summary of Twelfth Discourse

The twelfth discourse indicates that the path of devotion is easier than the path of knowledge. In this path the aspirant worships God in His Cosmic Form of the Supreme Personality. He develops a loving relationship with Him, adores Him, remembers Him and chants His glories and Name. He thus effects union with the Lord and attains not only His formless aspect but also the Lord as the manifest universe. The path of knowledge, whereby the aspirant meditates on the formless Brahman, is more difficult as he has to give up his attachment to the body from the very beginning. He has to have dispassion for the things of the world. How to practise devotion? Krishna asks Arjuna to fix his entire mind on Him. As often as the mind wanders it should be brought back to the Lord. If this process of concentration is difficult he should dedicate all his actions to Him, feeling that it is His power that activates everything. If this also is beyond his ability, he should offer all his actions to the Lord, abandoning the desire for their fruits. He should take complete refuge in Him. The devotee who surrenders himself to the Lord attains perfect peace. The Lord goes on to describe the qualities that a true devotee possesses. He neither attaches himself to anything nor does he have any aversion to things. He has a balanced mind under all 95 BHAGAVAD GITA circumstances. He is not agitated by the happenings of the world, nor does he himself cause any agitation in others. He is perfectly desireless and rejoices in the Lord within. He sees equality everywhere, being untouched by sorrow, fear, honour as also dishonour. He is perfectly content as he has surrendered his entire being to the Lord. Arjuna Uvaacha: Evam satatayuktaa ye bhaktaastwaam paryupaasate; Ye chaapyaksharamavyaktam teshaam ke yogavittamaah. Arjuna said: 1. Those devotees who, ever steadfast, thus worship Thee and those also who worship the Imperishable and the Unmanifested—which of them are better versed in Yoga? COMMENTARY: The twelfth discourse indicates that Bhakti Yoga is much easier than Jnana Yoga or the Yoga of knowledge. Sri Bhagavaan Uvaacha: Mayyaaveshya mano ye maam nityayuktaa upaasate; Shraddhayaa parayopetaaste me yuktatamaa mataah. The Blessed Lord said: 2. Those who, fixing their minds on Me, worship Me, ever steadfast and endowed with supreme faith, these are the best in Yoga in My opinion. Ye twaksharamanirdeshyamavyaktam paryupaasate; Sarvatragamachintyam cha kootasthamachalam dhruvam. 3. Those who worship the imperishable, the indefinable, the unmanifested, the omnipresent, the unthinkable, the eternal and the immovable, Samniyamyendriyagraamam sarvatra samabuddhayah; Te praapnuvanti maameva sarvabhootahite rataah. 4. Having restrained all the senses, even-minded everywhere, intent on the welfare of all beings—verily they also come unto Me. Klesho'dhikatarasteshaam avyaktaasaktachetasaam; Avyaktaa hi gatirduhkham dehavadbhiravaapyate. 5. Greater is their trouble whose minds are set on the Unmanifested; for the goal—the Unmanifested—is very difficult for the embodied to reach. COMMENTARY: The embodied—those who identify themselves with their bodies. The imperishable Self is very hard to reach for those who are attached to their bodies. Their restless minds will not be able to get fixed on the attributeless Self. Ye tu sarvaani karmaani mayi sannyasya matparaah; Ananyenaiva yogena maam dhyaayanta upaasate. 6. But to those who worship Me, renouncing all actions in Me, regarding Me as the supreme goal, meditating on Me with single-minded Yoga, Teshaamaham samuddhartaa mrityusamsaarasaagaraat; Bhavaami nachiraat paartha mayyaaveshitachetasaam. 7. To those whose minds are set on Me, O Arjuna, verily I become ere long the saviour out of the ocean of the mortal Samsara! Mayyeva mana aadhatswa mayi buddhim niveshaya; Nivasishyasi mayyeva ata oordhwam na samshayah. 8. Fix thy mind on Me only, thy intellect in Me, (then) thou shait no doubt live in Me alone hereafter. Atha chittam samaadhaatum na shaknoshi mayi sthiram; Abhyaasayogena tato maamicchaaptum dhananjaya. 9. If thou art unable to fix thy mind steadily on Me, then by the Yoga of constant practice do thou seek to reach Me, O Arjuna! Abhyaase'pyasamartho'si matkarmaparamo bhava; Madarthamapi karmaani kurvansiddhimavaapsyasi. 10. If thou art unable to practise even this Abhyasa Yoga, be thou intent on doing actions for My sake; even by doing actions for My sake, thou shalt attain perfection.

Athaitadapyashakto'si kartum madyogamaashritah; Sarvakarmaphalatyaagam tatah kuru yataatmavaan. 11. If thou art unable to do even this, then, taking refuge in union with Me, renounce the fruits of all actions with the self controlled. Shreyo hi jnaanamabhyaasaat jnaanaaddhyaanam vishishyate; Dhyaanaat karmaphalatyaagas tyaagaacchaantir anantaram. 12. Better indeed is knowledge than practice; than knowledge meditation is better; than meditation the renunciation of the fruits of actions; peace immediately follows renunciation. 97 BHAGAVAD GITA Adweshtaa sarvabhootaanaam maitrah karuna eva cha; Nirmamo nirahankaarah samaduhkhasukhah kshamee. 13. He who hates no creature, who is friendly and compassionate to all, who is free from attachment and egoism, balanced in pleasure and pain, and forgiving, Santushtah satatam yogee yataatmaa dridhanishchayah; Mayyarpitamanobuddhiryo madbhaktah sa me priyah. 14. Ever content, steady in meditation, possessed of firm conviction, self-controlled, with mind and intellect dedicated to Me, he, My devotee, is dear to Me. Yasmaannodwijate loko lokaannodwijate cha yah; Harshaamarshabhayodwegairmukto yah sa cha me priyah. 15. He by whom the world is not agitated and who cannot be agitated by the world, and who is freed from joy, envy, fear and anxiety—he is dear to Me. Anapekshah shuchirdaksha udaaseeno gatavyathah; Sarvaarambhaparityaagee yo madbhaktah sa me priyah. 16. He who is free from wants, pure, expert, unconcerned, and untroubled, renouncing all undertakings or commencements—he who is (thus) devoted to Me, is dear to Me. Yona hrishyati na dweshti na shochati na kaangkshati; Shubhaashubhaparityaagee bhaktimaan yah sa me priyah. 17. He who neither rejoices, nor hates, nor grieves, nor desires, renouncing good and evil, and who is full of devotion, is dear to Me. COMMENTARY: He does not rejoice when he attains desirable objects nor does he grieve when he parts with his cherished objects. Further, he does not desire the unattained. Samah shatrau cha mitre cha tathaa maanaapamaanayoh; Sheetoshnasukhaduhkheshu samah sangavivarjitah. 18. He who is the same to foe and friend, and in honour and dishonour, who is the same in cold and heat and in pleasure and pain, who is free from attachment, Tulyanindaastutirmaunee santushto yena kenachit: Aniketah sthiramatir bhaktimaan me priyo narah. 19. He to whom censure and praise are equal, who is silent, content with anything, homeless, of a steady mind, and full of devotion—that man is dear to Me. Ye tu dharmyaamritamidam yathoktam paryupaasate; 98 THE YOGA OF

DEVOTION Shraddhadhaanaah matparamaa bhaktaaste'teeva me priyaah. 20. They verily who follow this immortal Dharma (doctrine or law) as described above, endowed with faith, regarding Me as their supreme goal, they, the devotees, are exceedingly dear to Me. Hari Om Tat Sat Iti Srimad Bhagavadgeetaasoopanishatsu Brahmavidyaayaam Yogashaastre Sri Krishnaarjunasamvaade Bhaktiyogo Naama Dwaadasho'dhyaayah

DISTINCTION BETWEEN THE FIELD & THE KNOWER OF THE FIELD Summary of Thirteenth Discourse

In this discourse we have one of the most significant, most illuminating, most inspiring and most mystical portions of the Bhagavad Gita. The Lord gives us a wonderfully revealing insight into the human individual. It is the metaphysics of man, the unknown. The immortal Soul, with its physical embodiment, is the main theme of this discourse. The supreme transcendental Spirit, which is the eternal substratum beyond both, is also described in a wonderful manner. The knower of the Supreme Reality is instantly liberated. The blessed Lord tells us that the knowledge of the Field and the Knower of the Field is the true knowledge. This highest and the best knowledge grants us divine wisdom and spiritual illumination that lead to divine beatitude. This body is the Field. The Immortal Soul (yourself), dwelling in the body is the Knower of the Field. Verily, it is the Supreme Being who has projected Himself and assumed the form of this Knower of the Field within this body. This self is none other than That. Thus, Lord Krishna explains the mystery of the individual soul dwelling within this mortal body. This knowledge constitutes the main subject matter of all the scriptures and the highest philosophical works. The five elements, the ego, the mind, intellect and the ten organs, desire and aversion and such factors constitute the Field. Next follows a wonderful summing-up of what constitutes true knowledge. Then follows the declaration of the Supreme Soul, the knowledge of which grants us immortality. That Supreme Reality is the one universal Essence present everywhere. It pervades all. It shines within the inmost chambers of our heart, it is everything, it is the one seer, the witness, the guide, sustainer, experiencer and Lord of all. One who knows this mystery is not bound by activity 99 BHAGAVAD GITA even in the midst of life. When we perceive this supreme Presence dwelling in all beings we cannot injure anyone. Krishna asks us to see and know the difference between the Field (body or Prakriti) and the Knower of the Field (Spirit or Purusha), and thus reach the Self. This is the teaching and the message of this illuminating discourse. Arjuna Uvaacha: Prakritim purusham chaiva kshetram kshetrajnameva cha; Etadveditumicchaami jnaanam jneyam cha keshava. Arjuna said: 1. I wish to learn about Nature (matter) and the Spirit (soul), the Field and the Knower of the Field, knowledge and that which ought to be known. Sri Bhagavaan Uvaacha: Idam shareeram kaunteya kshetramityabhidheeyate; Etadyo vetti tam praahuh kshetrajna iti tadvidah. The Blessed Lord said: 2. This body, O Arjuna, is called the Field; he who knows it is called the Knower of the Field by those who know of them, that is, by the sages. Kshetrajnam chaapi maam viddhi sarvakshetreshu bhaarata; Kshetrakshetrajnayor jnaanam yattat jnaanam matam mama. 3. Do thou also know Me as the Knower of the Field in all fields, O Arjuna! Knowledge of both the Field and the Knower of the Field is considered by Me to be the knowledge. Tat kshetram yaccha yaadrik cha yadvikaari yatashcha yat; Sa cha yo yatprabhaavashcha tatsamaasena me shrinu. 4. What the Field is and of what nature, what its modifications are and whence it is, and also who He is and what His powers are—hear all that from Me in brief. Rishibhirbahudhaa geetam cchandobhirvividhaih prithak; Brahmasootrapadaishchaiva hetumadbhirvinishchitaih. 5. Sages have sung in many ways, in various distinctive chants and also in the suggestive words indicative of the Absolute, full of reasoning and decisive. Mahaabhootaanyahankaaro buddhiravyaktameva cha; Indriyaani dashaikam cha pancha chendriyagocharaah. 100 THE YOGA OF DISTINCTION BETWEEN THE FIELD & THE KNOWER OF THE FIELD 6. The great elements, egoism, intellect and also unmanifested Nature, the ten senses and one, and the five objects of the senses, COMMENTARY: Great elements: earth, water, fire, air and ether are so called because they pervade all modifications of matter. The ten senses are: the five organs of knowledge (ears, skin, eyes, tongue and nose), and the five organs of action (hand, feet, mouth, anus and generative organ). The one: this is the mind. The five objects of the senses are sound, touch, form colour, taste and smell. Icchaa dweshah sukham duhkham sanghaatashchetanaa dhritih; Etat kshetram samaasena savikaaramudaahritam. 7. Desire, hatred, pleasure, pain, the aggregate (the body), fortitude and intelligence—the Field has thus been described briefly with its modifications. Amaanitwam adambhitwam ahimsaa kshaantiraarjavam; Aachaaryopaasanam shaucham sthairyamaatmavinigrahah. 8. Humility, unpretentiousness, non-injury, forgiveness, uprightness, service of the teacher, purity, steadfastness, self-control, Indriyaartheshu vairaagyamanahankaara eva cha; Janmamrityujaraavyaadhi duhkhadoshaanu darshanam. 9. Indifference to the objects of the senses, also absence of egoism, perception of (or reflection on) the evil in birth, death, old age, sickness and pain, Asaktiranabhishwangah putradaaragrihaadishu; Nityam cha samachittatwam ishtaanishtopapattishu. 10. Non-attachment, non-identification of the Self with son, wife, home and the rest, and constant even-mindedness on the attainment of the desirable and the undesirable, Mayi chaananyayogena bhaktiravyabhichaarinee; Viviktadesha sevitwam aratir janasamsadi. 11. Unswerving devotion unto Me by the Yoga of non-separation, resort to solitary places, distaste for the society of men, Adhyaatma jnaana nityatwam tattwa jnaanaartha darshanam; Etajjnaanamiti proktam ajnaanam yadato'nyathaa. 12. Constancy in Self-knowledge, perception of the end of true knowledge—this is declared to be knowledge, and what is opposed to it is ignorance. 101 BHAGAVAD GITA Jneyam yattat pravakshyaami yajjnaatwaa'mritamashnute; Anaadimatparam brahma na sattannaasaduchyate. 13. I will declare that which has to be known, knowing which one attains to immortality, the beginningless supreme Brahman, called neither being nor non-being. Sarvatah paanipaadam tat sarvato'kshishiromukham; Sarvatah shrutimalloke sarvamaavritya tishthati. 14. With hands and feet everywhere, with eyes, heads and mouths everywhere, with ears everywhere, He exists in the worlds, enveloping all. Sarvendriyagunaabhaasam sarvendriyavivarjitam; Asaktam sarvabhricchaiva nirgunam gunabhoktru cha. 15. Shining by the functions of all the senses, yet without the senses; unattached, yet supporting all; devoid of qualities, yet their experiencer, Bahirantashcha bhootaanaam acharam charameva cha; Sookshmatwaat tadavijneyam doorastham chaantike cha tat. 16. Without and within (all) beings, the unmoving and also the moving; because of His subtlety, unknowable; and near and far away is That. Avibhaktam cha bhooteshu vibhaktamiva cha sthitam; Bhootabhartru cha tajjneyam grasishnu prabhavishnu cha. 17. And undivided, yet He exists as if divided in beings; He is to be known as the supporter of beings; He devours and He generates also. Jyotishaamapi tajjyotistamasah paramuchyate; Jnaanam jneyam jnaanagamyam hridi sarvasya vishthitam. 18. That, the Light of all lights, is beyond darkness; it is said to be knowledge, the Knowable and the goal of knowledge, seated in the hearts of all. Iti kshetram tathaa jnaanam jneyam choktam samaasatah; Madbhakta etadvijnaaya madbhaavaayopapadyate. 19. Thus the Field as well as knowledge and the Knowable have been briefly stated. My devotee, knowing this, enters into My Being. Prakritim purusham chaiva viddhyaanaadee ubhaavapi; Vikaaraamshcha gunaamshchaiva viddhi prakritisambhavaan. 102 THE YOGA OF DISTINCTION BETWEEN THE FIELD & THE KNOWER OF THE FIELD 20. Know thou that Nature and Spirit are beginningless; and know also that all modifications and qualities are born of Nature. Kaaryakaaranakartrutwe hetuh prakritiruchyate; Purushah sukhaduhkhaanaam bhoktritwe heturuchyate. 21. In the production of the effect and the cause, Nature (matter) is said to be the cause; in the experience of pleasure and pain, the soul is said to be the cause. Purushah prakritistho hi bhungkte prakritijaan gunaan; Kaaranam gunasango'sya sadasadyoni janmasu. 22. The soul seated in Nature experiences the qualities born of Nature; attachment to the qualities is the cause of his birth in good and evil wombs. Upadrashtaanumantaa cha bhartaa bhoktaa maheshwarah; Paramaatmeti chaapyukto dehe'smin purushah parah. 23. The Supreme Soul in this body is also called the spectator, the permitter, the supporter, the enjoyer, the great Lord and the Supreme Self. Ya evam vetti purusham prakritim cha gunaih saha; Sarvathaa vartamaano'pi na sa bhooyo'bhijaayate. 24. He who thus knows Spirit and Matter, together with the qualities, in whatever condition he may be, he is not reborn. Dhyaanenaatmani pashyanti kechidaatmaanamaatmanaa; Anye saankhyena yogena karmayogena chaapare. 25. Some by meditation behold the Self in the Self by the Self, others by the Yoga of knowledge, and others by the Yoga of action. Anye twevamajaanantah shrutwaanyebhya upaasate; Te'pi chaatitarantyeva mrityum shrutiparaayanaah. 26. Others also, not knowing thus, worship, having heard of it from others; they, too, cross beyond death, regarding what they have heard as the supreme refuge. Yaavat sanjaayate kinchit sattwam sthaavarajangamam;

Kshetrakshetrajnasamyogaat tadviddhi bharatarshabha. 27. Wherever a being is born, whether it be unmoving or moving, know thou, O best of the Bharatas (Arjuna), that it is from the union between the Field and its Knower. Samam sarveshu bhooteshu tishthantam parameshwaram; 103 BHAGAVAD GITA Vinashyatswavinashyantam yah pashyati sa pashyati. 28. He sees, who sees the Supreme Lord, existing equally in all beings, the unperishing within the perishing. COMMENTARY: Birth is the root cause of the modifications of change, growth, decay and death. The other changes of state manifest after the birth of the body. But the Lord is changeless and He is birthless, decayless and deathless. Samam pashyan hi sarvatra samavasthitameeshwaram; Na hinastyaatmanaa'tmaanam tato yaati paraam gatim. 29. Because he who sees the same Lord dwelling equally everywhere does not destroy the Self by the self, he goes to the highest goal. Prakrityaiva cha karmaani kriyamaanaani sarvashah; Yah pashyati tathaa'tmaanam akartaaram sa pashyati. 30. He sees, who sees that all actions are performed by Nature alone and that the Self is actionless. Yadaa bhootaprithagbhaavam ekastham anupashyati; Tata eva cha vistaaram brahma sampadyate tadaa. 31. When a man sees the whole variety of beings as resting in the One, and spreading forth from That alone, he then becomes Brahman. COMMENTARY: A man attains to unity with the Supreme when he knows or realises through intuition that all these manifold forms are rooted in the One. Like waves in water, like rays in the sun, so also all forms are rooted in the One. Anaaditwaan nirgunatwaat paramaatmaayam avyayah; Shareerastho'pi kaunteya na karoti na lipyate. 32. Being without beginning and devoid of (any) qualities, the Supreme Self, imperishable, though dwelling in the body, O Arjuna, neither acts nor is tainted! Yathaa sarvagatam saukshmyaadaakaasham nopalipyate; Sarvatraavasthito dehe tathaatmaa nopalipyate. 33. As the all-pervading ether is not tainted because of its subtlety, so the Self seated everywhere in the body, is not tainted. Yathaa prakaashayatyekah kritsnam lokamimam ravih; Kshetram kshetree tathaa kritsnam prakaashayati bhaarata. 104 THE YOGA OF DISTINCTION BETWEEN THE FIELD & THE KNOWER OF THE FIELD 34. Just as the one sun illumines the whole world, so also the Lord of the Field (the Supreme Self) illumines the whole Field, O Arjuna! Kshetrakshetrajnayor evam antaram jnaanachakshushaa; Bhootaprakritimoksham cha ye vidur yaanti te param. 35. They who, through the eye of knowledge, perceive the distinction between the Field and its Knower, and also the liberation from the Nature of being, they go to the Supreme. COMMENTARY: They who know through the eye of intuition opened by meditation and the instructions of the Guru and the scriptures, that the Field is insentient, the doer, changing and finite, and that the Knower of the Field is pure Consciousness, the non-doer, unchanging and infinite, and who also perceive the non-existence of Nature, ignorance, the Unmanifested, the material cause of being,—they attain the Supreme.

CHAPTER EIGHTEEN

THE DIVISION OF THE THREE GUNAS Summary of Fourteenth Discourse

Knowledge of the three cosmic qualities or Gunas, namely, Sattwa, Rajas and Tamas is now given through this discourse. The knowledge of these three Gunas, which hold the entire universe and all creatures under their sway, is of vital importance to each and everyone for their progress and happiness in life. Without this knowledge one will be forever bound by sorrow. In this knowledge we have the secret of success in worldly life as well as in spiritual life. Therefore, one should acquire this precious knowledge. Lord Krishna reveals that these three qualities compose the Cosmic Nature. This Cosmic Nature is the primal source and origin of the entire creation and all things in it. Hence all things created are subject to their influence and irresistible power. The individual soul also is bound to the body by these three qualities present in Cosmic Nature. The Supreme Being brings about creation through the help of His Prakriti (Nature) endowed with these threefold qualities. 105 BHAGAVAD GITA The highest of the three qualities is Sattwa. It is pure. It brings about happiness, wisdom and also illumination. The second quality of Rajas gives rise to passion manifested by intense attachment and greed. It causes sorrow and suffering. The third, termed Tamas, is the worst of all. It arises due to ignorance and results in darkness, lethargy and delusion. Krishna asks us to diligently endeavour to cast out Tamas from our nature. We should control and master Rajas, and by holding it in check, wisely divert its power towards good kinds of activities. Sattwa should be carefully cultivated, developed and conserved in order to enable us to attain immortality. The realised sage, of course, goes beyond all these qualities, for, although it is Sattwa that enables him to reach God, even this quality will bind him if he is attached to it. The aspirant should know the symptoms and signs of their presence in his personality and acquire a knowledge of their subtle workings. Then only can he maintain an unhampered and smooth progress in all activities of his life, both secular as well as spiritual. Lord Krishna teaches us this important subject in this discourse from the ninth to the eighteenth verse. He declares that one who rises beyond all the three Gunas through spiritual practices, becomes free from birth, death, old age and sorrow, and enjoys immortality. In reply to a question from Arjuna, the blessed Lord describes the marks of one who has risen above the three Gunas. He states that if one constantly worships Him with exclusive devotion one will attain the highest divine experience and supreme peace and blessedness. Sri Bhagavaan Uvaacha: Param bhooyah pravakshyaami jnaanaanaam jnaanamuttamam; Yajjnaatwaa munayah sarve paraam siddhimito gataah. The Blessed Lord said: 1. I will again declare (to thee) that supreme knowledge, the best of all knowledge, having known which all the sages have gone to the supreme perfection after this life. Idam jnaanam upaashritya mama saadharmyam aagataah; Sarge'pi nopajaayante pralaye na vyathanti cha. 2. They who, having taken refuge in this knowledge, attain to unity with Me, are neither born at the time of creation nor are they disturbed at the time of dissolution. COMMENTARY: In this verse it is knowledge of the Supreme Self that is eulogised by the Lord. Mama yonirmahadbrahma tasmin garbham dadhaamyaham; Sambhavah sarvabhootaanaam tato bhavati bhaarata. 3. My womb is the great Brahma; in that I place the germ; thence, O Arjuna, is the birth of all beings! 106 THE YOGA OF THE DIVISION OF THE THREE GUNAS Sarvayonishu kaunteya moortayah sambhavanti yaah; Taasaam brahma mahadyonir aham beejapradah pitaa. 4. Whatever forms are produced, O Arjuna, in any womb whatsoever, the great Brahma is their womb and I am the seed-giving father. Sattwam rajastama iti gunaah prakriti sambhavaah; Nibadhnanti mahaabaaho dehe dehinam avyayam. 5. Purity, passion and inertia—these qualities, O mighty-armed Arjuna, born of Nature, bind fast in the body, the embodied, the indestructible! COMMENTARY: The three Gunas are present in all human beings. None is free from the operation of any one of the three qualities. They are not constant. Sometimes Sattwa predominates and at other times Rajas or Tamas predominates. One should analyse and stand as a witness of these three qualities. Tatra sattwam nirmalatwaat prakaashakam anaamayam; Sukhasangena badhnaati jnaanasangena chaanagha. 6. Of these, Sattwa, which from its stainlessness is luminous and healthy, binds by attachment to knowledge and to happiness, O sinless one! Rajo raagaatmakam viddhi trishnaasangasamudbhavam; Tannibadhnaati kaunteya karmasangena dehinam. 7. Know thou Rajas to be of the nature of passion, the source of thirst (for sensual enjoyment) and attachment; it binds fast, O Arjuna, the embodied one by attachment to action! Tamastwajnaanajam viddhi mohanam sarvadehinaam; Pramaadaalasyanidraabhis tannibadhnaati bhaarata. 8. But know thou Tamas to be born of ignorance, deluding all embodied beings; it binds fast, O Arjuna, by heedlessness, sleep and indolence! Sattwam sukhe sanjayati rajah karmani bhaarata; Jnaanamaavritya tu tamah pramaade sanjayatyuta. 9. Sattwa attaches to happiness, Rajas to action, O Arjuna, while Tamas, shrouding knowledge, attaches to heedlessness only! Rajastamashchaabhibhooya sattwam bhavati bhaarata; Rajah sattwam tamashchaiva tamah sattwam rajastathaa. 10. Now Sattwa prevails, O Arjuna, having overpowered Rajas and Tamas; now Rajas, having overpowered Sattwa and Tamas; and now Tamas, having overpowered Sattwa and Rajas! 107 BHAGAVAD GITA Sarvadwaareshu dehe'smin prakaasha upajaayate; Jnaanam yadaa tadaa vidyaa dvivriddham sattwamityuta. 11. When, through every gate (sense) in this body, the wisdom-light shines, then it may be known that Sattwa is predominant. Lobhah pravrittir aarambhah karmanaam ashamah sprihaa; Rajasyetaani jaayante vivriddhe bharatarshabha. 12. Greed, activity, the undertaking of actions, restlessness, longing—these arise when Rajas is predominant, O Arjuna! Aprakaasho'pravrittishcha pramaado moha eva cha; Tamasyetaani jaayante vivriddhe kurunandana. 13. Darkness, inertness, heedlessness and delusion—these arise when Tamas is predominant, O Arjuna! Yadaa sattwe pravriddhe tu pralayam yaati dehabhrit; Tadottamavidaam lokaan amalaan pratipadyate. 14. If the embodied one meets with death when Sattwa has become predominant, then he attains to the spotless worlds of the knowers of the Highest. Rajasi pralayam gatwaa karmasangishu jaayate; Tathaa praleenastamasi moodhayonishu jaayate. 15. Meeting death in Rajas, he is born among those who are attached to action; and dying in Tamas, he is born in the womb of the senseless. Karmanah sukritasyaahuh saattwikam nirmalam phalam; Rajasastu phalam duhkham ajnaanam tamasah phalam. 16. The fruit of good action, they say, is Sattwic and pure; the fruit of Rajas is pain, and ignorance is the fruit of Tamas. Sattwaat sanjaayate jnaanam rajaso lobha eva cha; Pramaadamohau tamaso bhavato'jnaanameva cha. 17. From

Sattwa arises knowledge, and greed from Rajas; heedlessness and delusion arise from Tamas, and ignorance also. Oordhwam gacchanti sattwasthaa madhye tishthanti raajasaah; Jaghanyagunavrittisthaa adho gacchanti taamasaah. 108 THE YOGA OF THE DIVISION OF THE THREE GUNAS 18. Those who are seated in Sattwa proceed upwards; the Rajasic dwell in the middle; and the Tamasic, abiding in the function of the lowest Guna, go downwards. Naanyam gunebhyah kartaaram yadaa drashtaanupashyati; Gunebhyashcha param vetti madbhaavam so'dhigacchati. 19. When the seer beholds no agent other than the Gunas, knowing that which is higher than them, he attains to My Being. COMMENTARY: The seer knows that the Gunas alone are responsible for all actions and He is distinct from them. Gunaanetaanateetya treen dehee dehasamudbhavaan; Janmamrityujaraaduhkhair vimukto'mritamashnute. 20. The embodied one, having crossed beyond these three Gunas out of which the body is evolved, is freed from birth, death, decay and pain, and attains to immortality. Arjuna Uvaacha: Kairlingais treen gunaanetaan ateeto bhavati prabho; Kimaachaarah katham chaitaam streen gunaan ativartate. Arjuna said: 21. What are the marks of him who has crossed over the three qualities, O Lord? What is his conduct and how does he go beyond these three qualities? Sri Bhagavaan Uvaacha: Prakaasham cha pravrittim cha mohameva cha paandava; Na dweshti sampravrittaani na nivrittaani kaangkshati. The Blessed Lord said: 22. Light, activity and delusion,—when they are present, O Arjuna, he hates not, nor does he long for them when they are absent! Udaaseenavadaaseeno gunairyo na vichaalyate; Gunaa vartanta ityeva yo'vatishthati nengate. 23. He who, seated like one unconcerned, is not moved by the qualities, and who, knowing that the qualities are active, is self-centred and moves not, Samaduhkhasukhah swasthah samaloshtaashmakaanchanah; Tulyapriyaapriyo dheeras tulyanindaatma samstutih. 109 BHAGAVAD GITA 24. Alike in pleasure and pain, who dwells in the Self, to whom a clod of earth, stone and gold are alike, to whom the dear and the unfriendly are alike, firm, the same in censure and praise, Maanaapamaanayostulyas tulyo mitraaripakshayoh; Sarvaarambhaparityaagee gunaateetah sa uchyate. 25. The same in honour and dishonour, the same to friend and foe, abandoning all undertakings—he is said to have crossed the qualities. Maam cha yo'vyabhichaarena bhaktiyogena sevate; Sa gunaan samateetyaitaan brahmabhooyaaya kalpate. 26. And he who serves Me with unswerving devotion, he, crossing beyond the qualities, is fit for becoming Brahman. Brahmano hi pratishthaa'ham amritasyaavyayasya cha; Shaashwatasya cha dharmasya sukhasyaikaantikasya cha. 27. For I am the abode of Brahman, the immortal and the immutable, of everlasting Dharma and of absolute bliss. Hari Om Tat Sat Iti Srimad Bhagavadgeetaasoopanishatsu Brahmavidyaayaam Yogashaastre Sri Krishnaarjunasamvaade Gunatrayavibhaagayogo Naama Chaturdasho'dhyaayah Thus in the Upanishads of the glorious Bhagavad Gita, the science of the Eternal, the scripture of Yoga, the dialogue between Sri Krishna and Arjuna, ends the fourteenth discourse entitled.

CHAPTER NINETEEN

THE SUPREME SPIRIT
Summary of Fifteenth Discourse

This discourse is entitled "Purushottama Yoga" or the "Yoga of the Supreme Person". Here Lord Krishna tells us about the ultimate source of this visible phenomenal universe from which all things have come into being, just like a great tree with all its roots, trunk, branches, twigs, leaves, flowers and fruits which spring forth from the earth, which itself supports the tree and in which it is rooted. Sri Krishna declares that the Supreme Being is the source of all existence, and refers allegorically to this universe as being like an inverted tree whose roots are in Para Brahman, and whose spreading branches and foliage constitute all the things and factors that go to make up this 110 THE YOGA OF THE DIVISION OF THE THREE GUNAS creation of variegated phenomena. This is a very mysterious "Tree" which is very difficult to understand, being a product of His inscrutable power of Maya; and hence a marvellous, apparent appearance without having actual reality. One who fully understands the nature of this Samsara-Tree goes beyond Maya. To be attached to it is to be caught in it. The surest way of transcending this Samsara or worldly life is by wielding the excellent weapon of dispassion and non-attachment. In verses four and five of this discourse the Lord tells us how one goes beyond this visible Samsara and attains the supreme, imperishable status, attaining which one does not have to return to this mortal world of pain and death. Lord Krishna also describes for us the wonderful mystery of His Presence in this universe and the supreme place He occupies in sustaining everything here. The Lord declares that it is a part of Himself that manifests here as the individual soul in each body. He Himself is the indwelling Oversoul beyond the self. He is the effulgence inherent in the sun, moon and fire. He is present as the nourishing element in the earth. He is the inner witness of all beings. He is the supreme Knower even beyond Vedic knowledge. He is the resplendent Person who is beyond both this perishable phenomenal creation as well as the imperishable individual soul which is a part of His eternal essence. Thus, because He is beyond perishable matter and superior to the imperishable soul (enveloped in Maya), He is known in this world as well as in the Vedas as the Supreme Person. Sri Bhagavaan Uvaacha: Oordhwamoolam adhahshaakham ashwattham praahuravyayam; Cchandaamsi yasya parnaani yastam veda sa vedavit. The Blessed Lord said: 1. They (the wise) speak of the indestructible peepul tree, having its root above and branches below, whose leaves are the metres or hymns; he who knows it is a knower of the Vedas. Adhashchordhwam prasritaastasya shaakhaah Gunapravriddhaa vishayapravaalaah; Adhashcha moolaanyanusantataani Karmaanubandheeni manushyaloke. 2. Below and above spread its branches, nourished by the Gunas; sense-objects are its buds; and below in the world of men stretch forth the roots, originating action. Na roopamasyeha tathopalabhyate Naanto na chaadirna cha sampratishthaa; Ashwatthamenam suviroodhamoolam Asangashastrena dridhena cchittwaa. 111 BHAGAVAD GITA 3. Its form is not perceived here as such, neither its end nor its origin, nor its foundation nor resting place; having cut asunder this firmly-rooted peepul tree with the strong axe of non-attachment, Tatah padam tat parimaargitavyam Yasmin gataa na nivartanti bhooyah; Tameva chaadyam purusham prapadye Yatah pravrittih prasritaa puraanee. 4. Then that goal should be sought after, whither having gone none returns again. Seek refuge in that Primeval Purusha whence streamed forth the ancient activity or energy. COMMENTARY: That which fills the whole world with the form of Satchidananda, is Purusha. That which sleeps in this city of the body is the Purusha. Single-minded devotion, which consists of ceaselessly remembering the Supreme Being, is the surest and most potent means of attaining Self-realisation. Nirmaanamohaa jitasangadoshaa Adhyaatmanityaa vinivrittakaamaah; Dwandwairvimuktaah sukhaduhkhasamjnair Gacchantyamoodhaah padamavyayam tat. 5. Free from pride and delusion, victorious over the evil of attachment, dwelling constantly in the Self, their desires having completely turned away, freed from the pairs of opposites known as pleasure and pain, the undeluded reach the eternal goal. Na tadbhaasayate sooryo na shashaangko na paavakah; Yadgatwaa na nivartante taddhaama paramam mama. 6. Neither doth the sun illumine there, nor the moon, nor the fire; having gone thither they return not; that is My supreme abode. Mamaivaamsho jeevaloke jeevabhootah sanaatanah; Manah shashthaaneendriyaani prakritisthaani karshati. 7. An eternal portion of Myself having become a living soul in the world of life, draws to (itself) the (five) senses with the mind for the sixth, abiding in Nature. Shareeram yadavaapnoti yacchaapyutkraamateeshwarah; Griheetwaitaani samyaati vaayurgandhaanivaashayaat. 8. When the Lord obtains a body and when He leaves it, He takes these and goes (with them) as the wind takes the scents from their seats (flowers, etc.). Shrotram chakshuh sparshanam cha rasanam ghraanameva cha; Adhishthaaya manashchaayam vishayaanupasevate. 112 THE YOGA OF THE SUPREME SPIRIT 9. Presiding over the ear, the eye, touch, taste and smell, as well as the mind, he enjoys the objects of the senses. Utkraamantam sthitam vaapi bhunjaanam vaa gunaanvitam; Vimoodhaa naanupashyanti pashyanti jnaanachakshushah. 10. The deluded do not see Him who departs, stays and enjoys; but they who possess the eye of knowledge behold Him. Yatanto yoginashchainam pashyantyaatmanyavasthitam; Yatanto'pyakritaatmaano nainam pashyantyachetasah. 11. The Yogis striving (for perfection) behold Him dwelling in the Self; but, the unrefined and unintelligent, even though striving, see Him not. Yadaadityagatam tejo jagad bhaasayate'khilam; Yacchandramasi yacchaagnau tattejo viddhi maamakam. 12. That light which residing in the sun, illumines the whole world, that which is in the moon and in the fire—know that light to be Mine. Gaam aavishya cha bhootaani dhaarayaamyaham ojasaa; Pushnaami chaushadheeh sarvaah somo bhootwaa rasaatmakah. 13. Permeating the earth I support all beings by (My) energy; and, having become the watery moon, I nourish all herbs. Aham vaishwaanaro bhootwaa praaninaam dehamaashritah; Praanaapaana samaayuktah pachaamyannam chaturvidham. 14. Having become the fire Vaisvanara, I abide in the body of living beings and, associated with the Prana and Apana, digest the fourfold food. Sarvasya chaaham hridi sannivishto Mattah smritir jnaanam apohanam cha; Vedaischa sarvairahameva vedyo Vedaantakrid vedavid eva chaaham. 15. And, I am seated in the hearts of all; from Me are memory, knowledge, as well as their absence. I am verily that which has to be known by all the Vedas; I am indeed the author of the Vedanta, and the knower of the Vedas am I. Dwaavimau purushau loke ksharashchaakshara eva cha; Ksharah sarvaani bhootaani kootastho'kshara uchyate. 113 BHAGAVAD GITA 16. Two Purushas there are in this world, the perishable and the imperishable. All beings are the perishable, and the Kutastha is called the imperishable. Uttamah purushastwanyah paramaatmetyudaahritah; Yo lokatrayamaavishya bibhartyavyaya ishwarah. 17. But distinct is the Supreme Purusha called the highest Self, the indestructible Lord who, pervading the three worlds, sustains them. Yasmaat ksharam ateeto'hamaksharaadapi chottamah; Ato'smi loke vede cha prathitah purushottamah. 18. As I transcend the perishable and am even higher than the imperishable, I am declared as the highest Purusha in the world and in the Vedas. Yo maamevam asammoodho jaanaati purushottamam; Sa sarvavidbhajati maam sarvabhaavena bhaarata. 19. He who, undeluded, knows Me thus as the highest Purusha, he, knowing all, worships Me with his whole being (heart), O Arjuna! Iti guhyatamam shaastram idamuktam mayaa'nagha; Etadbuddhwaa buddhimaan syaat kritakrityashcha bhaarata. 20. Thus, this most secret science has been taught by Me, O sinless one! On knowing this, a man becomes wise, and all his duties are accomplished, O Arjuna! Hari Om Tat Sat Iti Srimad Bhagavadgeetaasoopanishatsu Brahmavidyaayaam Yogashaastre Sri Krishnaarjunasamvaade Purushottamayogo Naama Panchadasho'dhyaayah Thus in the Upanishads of the glorious Bhagavad Gita, the science of the Eternal, the scripture of Yoga, the dialogue between Sri Krishna and Arjuna, ends the fifteenth discourse .

CHAPTER TWENTY

THE DIVISION BETWEEN THE DIVINE AND THE DEMONIACAL Summary of Sixteenth Discourse

This discourse is important and very instructive to all persons who wish to attain happiness, prosperity and blessedness, and to seekers in particular, who wish to attain success in their spiritual life. Lord Krishna brings out quite clearly and unmistakably here the intimate connection between ethics and spirituality, between a life of virtue and God-realisation and liberation. Listing two sets of qualities of opposite kinds, the Lord classifies them as divine and demoniacal (undivine), and urges us to eradicate the latter and cultivate the divine qualities. What kind of nature should one develop? What conduct must one follow? What way should one live and act if one must attain God and obtain divine bliss? These questions are answered with perfect clarity and very definitely. The pure divine qualities are conducive to peace and liberation and the undivine qualities lead to bondage. Purity, good conduct and truth are indispensable to spiritual progress and even to an honourable life here. Devoid of purity, good conduct and truth, and having no faith in God or a higher Reality beyond this visible world, man degenerates into a two-legged beast of ugly character and cruel actions, and sinks into darkness. Such a person becomes his own enemy and the destroyer of the happiness of others as well as his own. Caught in countless desires and cravings, a slave of sensual enjoyments and beset by a thousand cares, his life ultimately ends in misery and degradation. Haughtiness, arrogance and egoism lead to this dire fate. Therefore, a wise person, desiring success, must eradicate vice and cultivate virtue. In this world three gates lead to hell—the gates of passion, anger and greed. Released from these three qualities one can succeed in attaining salvation and reaching the highest goal, namely God. Thus the sacred scriptures teach wisely the right path of pure, virtuous living. One should therefore follow the injunctions of the sacred scriptures that wish his welfare and be guided in his actions by their noble teachings. Sri Bhagavaan Uvaacha: Abhayam sattwasamshuddhih jnaanayogavyavasthitih; Daanam damashcha yajnashcha swaadhyaayastapa aarjavam. The Blessed Lord said: 1. Fearlessness, purity of heart, steadfastness in Yoga and knowledge, alms-giving, control of the senses, sacrifice, study of scriptures, austerity and straightforwardness, Ahimsaa satyamakrodhas tyaagah shaantirapaishunam; 115 BHAGAVAD GITA Dayaa bhooteshvaloluptwam maardavam hreerachaapalam. 2. Harmlessness, truth, absence of anger, renunciation, peacefulness, absence of crookedness, compassion towards beings, uncovetousness, gentleness, modesty, absence of fickleness, Tejah kshamaa dhritih shauchamadroho naatimaanitaa; Bhavanti sampadam daiveem abhijaatasya bhaarata. 3. Vigour, forgiveness, fortitude, purity, absence of hatred, absence of pride—these belong to one born in a divine state, O Arjuna! Dambho darpo'bhimaanashcha krodhah paarushyameva cha; Ajnaanam chaabhijaatasya paartha sampadamaasureem. 4. Hypocrisy, arrogance, self-conceit, harshness and also anger and ignorance, belong to one who is born in a demoniacal state, O Arjuna! Daivee sampadvimokshaaya nibandhaayaasuree mataa; Maa shuchah sampadam daiveem abhijaato'si paandava. 5. The divine nature is deemed for liberation and the demoniacal for bondage. Grieve not, O Arjuna, for thou art born with divine properties! COMMENTARY: As Arjuna is dejected, Sri Krishna assures him not to feel alarmed at this description of the demoniacal qualities as he is born with Sattwic tendencies leading towards salvation. Dwau bhootasargau loke'smin daiva aasura eva cha; Daivo vistarashah proktah aasuram paartha me shrinu. 6. There are two types of beings in this world—the divine and the demoniacal; the divine has been described at length; hear from Me, O Arjuna, of the demoniacal! Pravrittim cha nivrittim cha janaa na viduraasuraah; Na shaucham naapi chaachaaro na satyam teshu vidyate. 7. The demoniacal know not what to do and what to refrain from; neither purity nor right conduct nor truth is found in them. Asatyamapratishtham te jagadaahuraneeshwaram; Aparasparasambhootam kimanyat kaamahaitukam. 8. They say: "This universe is without truth, without a (moral) basis, without a God, brought about by mutual union, with lust for its cause; what else?" 116 THE YOGA OF THE DIVISION BETWEEN THE DIVINE AND THE DEMONIACAL Etaam drishtimavashtabhya nashtaatmaano'lpabuddhayah; Prabhavantyugrakarmaanah kshayaaya jagato'hitaah. 9. Holding this view, these ruined souls of small intellects and fierce deeds, come forth as enemies of the world for its destruction. Kaamamaashritya dushpooram dambhamaanamadaanvitaah; Mohaadgriheetvaasadgraahaan pravartante'shuchivrataah. 10. Filled with insatiable desires, full of hypocrisy, pride and arrogance, holding evil ideas through delusion, they work with impure resolves. Chintaamaparimeyaam cha pralayaantaamupaashritaah; Kaamopabhogaparamaa etaavaditi nishchitaah. 11. Giving themselves over to immeasurable cares ending only with death, regarding gratification of lust as their highest aim, and feeling sure that that is all, Aashaapaashashatairbaddhaah kaamakrodhaparaayanaah; Eehante kaamabhogaartha manyaayenaarthasanchayaan. 12. Bound by a hundred ties of hope, given over to lust and anger, they strive to obtain by unlawful means hoards of wealth for sensual enjoyment. Idamadya mayaa labdham imam praapsye manoratham; Idamasteedamapi me bhavishyati punardhanam. 13. "This has been gained by me today; this desire I shall obtain; this is mine and this wealth too shall be mine in future." Asau mayaa hatah shatrur hanishye chaaparaanapi; Eeshwaro'hamaham bhogee siddho'ham balavaan sukhee. 14. "That enemy has been slain by me and others also I shall slay. I am the lord; I enjoy; I am perfect, powerful and happy". Aadhyo'bhijanavaanasmi ko'nyosti sadrisho mayaa; Yakshye daasyaami modishye ityajnaanavimohitaah. 15. "I am rich and born in a noble family. Who else is equal to me? I will sacrifice. I will give (charity). I will rejoice,"—thus, deluded by ignorance, Anekachittavibhraantaah mohajaalasamaavritaah; Prasaktaah kaamabhogeshu patanti narake'shuchau. 117 BHAGAVAD GITA 16. Bewildered by many a fancy, entangled in the snare of delusion, addicted to the gratification of lust, they fall into a foul hell. Aatmasambhaavitaah stabdhaa dhanamaanamadaanvitaah; Yajante naamayajnaiste dambhenaavidhipoorvakam. 17. Self-conceited, stubborn, filled with the intoxication and pride of wealth, they perform sacrifices in name, through ostentation, contrary to scriptural ordinances. Ahankaaram balam darpam kaamam krodham cha samshritaah; Maamaatmaparadeheshu pradwishanto'bhyasooyakaah. 18. Given over to egoism, power, haughtiness, lust and anger, these malicious people hate Me in their own bodies and those of others. Taanaham dwishatah krooraan samsaareshu naraadhamaan; Kshipaamyajasram ashubhaan aasureeshweva yonishu. 19. These cruel haters, the worst among men in the world,—I hurl all these evil-doers for ever into the wombs of demons only. Aasureem yonimaapannaa moodhaa janmani janmani; Maamapraapyaiva kaunteya tato yaantyadhamaam gatim. 20. Entering into demoniacal wombs and deluded birth after birth, not attaining Me, they thus fall, O Arjuna, into a condition still lower than that! Trividham narakasyedam dwaaram naashanamaatmanah; Kaamah krodhastathaa lobhas tasmaadetat trayam tyajet. 21. Triple is the gate of this hell, destructive of the self—lust, anger, and greed,—therefore, one should abandon these three. Etairvimuktah kaunteya tamodwaaraistribhirnarah; Aacharatyaatmanah shreyas tato yaati paraam gatim. 22. A man who is liberated from these three gates to darkness, O Arjuna, practises what is good for him and thus goes to the Supreme goal! COMMENTARY: When these three gates to hell are abandoned, the path to salvation is cleared for the aspirant. He gets the company of sages, which leads to liberation. He receives spiritual instructions and practises them. He hears the scriptures, reflects, meditates and attains Self-realisation. Yah shaastravidhimutsrijya vartate kaamakaaratah; Na sa siddhimavaapnoti na sukham na paraam gatim. 118 THE YOGA OF THE DIVISION BETWEEN THE DIVINE AND THE DEMONIACAL 23. He who, casting aside the ordinances of the scriptures, acts under the impulse of desire, attains neither perfection nor happiness nor the supreme goal. Tasmaat shaastram pramaanam te kaaryaakaaryavyavasthitau; Jnaatwaa shaastravidhaanoktam karma kartumihaarhasi. 24. Therefore, let the scripture be the authority in determining what ought to be done and what ought not to be done. Having known what is said in the ordinance of the scriptures, thou shouldst act here in this world.

CHAPTER TWENTY-ONE

THE DIVISION OF THE THREEFOLD FAITH Summary of Seventeenth Discourse

This discourse is termed the "Yoga of the Division of the Three Kinds of Faith". The theme of this discourse arises out of the question asked by Arjuna in Verse 1 with reference to the final and closing advice of Lord Krishna in the previous discourse, contained in the last two verses therein (Verses 23 and 24). Arjuna asks, "What about those who, even though setting aside scriptural injunctions yet perform worship with faith?" The Lord replies and states that the faith of such men who ignore the injunctions of the scriptures could be either Sattwic, Rajasic or Tamasic. This would be in accordance with the basic nature of the person himself. And, conversely, as is the kind of faith, so develops the nature of the man. Thus, in all things like sacrifice, worship, charity, penance, etc., these qualities become expressed in accordance with the kind of faith in which the person concerned is based. They produce results in accordance with the quality of the doer's faith. These acts done with right faith lead to supreme blessedness. When done without any faith whatsoever, all these actions become barren and useless.Arjuna Uvaacha: Ye shaastravidhimutsrijya yajante shraddhayaanvitaah; Teshaam nishthaa tu kaa krishna sattwamaaho rajastamah. Arjuna said: 1. Those who, setting aside the ordinances of the scriptures, perform sacrifice with faith, what is their condition, O Krishna? Is it that of Sattwa, Rajas or Tamas? COMMENTARY: This discourse deals with the three kinds of faith, according to one's inherent nature—Sattwic, Rajasic or Tamasic. Sri Bhagavaan Uvaacha: Trividhaa bhavati shraddhaa dehinaam saa swabhaavajaa; Saattwikee raajasee chaiva taamasee cheti taam shrinu. The Blessed Lord said: 2. Threefold is the faith of the embodied, which is inherent in their nature—the Sattwic (pure), the Rajasic (passionate), and the Tamasic (dark). Do thou hear of it. Sattwaanuroopaa sarvasya shraddhaa bhavati bhaarata; Shraddhaamayo'yam purusho yo yacchraddhah sa eva sah. 3. The faith of each is in accordance with his nature, O Arjuna! The man consists of his faith; as a man's faith is, so is he. Yajante saattwikaa devaan yaksharakshaamsi raajasaah; Pretaan bhootaganaamshchaanye yajante taamasaa janaah. 4. The Sattwic or pure men worship the gods; the Rajasic or the passionate worship the Yakshas and the Rakshasas; the others (the Tamasic or the deluded) worship the ghosts and the hosts of nature-spirits. Ashaastravihitam ghoram tapyante ye tapo janaah; Dambhaahamkaarasamyuktaah kaamaraagabalaanvitaah. 5. Those men who practise terrific austerities not enjoined by the scriptures, given to hypocrisy and egoism, impelled by the force of lust and attachment, Karshayantah shareerastham bhootagraamamachetasah; Maam chaivaantahshareerastham taanviddhyaasuranishchayaan. 6. Senseless, torturing all the elements in the body and Me also, who dwells in the body,—know thou these to be of demoniacal resolves. 120 THE YOGA OF THE DIVISION OF THE THREEFOLD FAITH Aahaarastwapi sarvasya trividho bhavati priyah; Yajnastapastathaa daanam teshaam bhedamimam shrinu. 7. The food also which is dear to each is threefold, as also sacrifice, austerity and alms-giving. Hear thou the distinction of these. COMMENTARY: A man's taste for a particular food is determined according to the Guna prevalent in him. Aayuh sattwabalaarogya sukha preetivi vardhanaah; Rasyaah snigdhaah sthiraa hridyaa aahaaraah saattwikapriyaah. 8. Foods which increase life, purity, strength, health, joy and cheerfulness, which are oleaginous and savoury, substantial and agreeable, are dear to the Sattwic people. Katvamlalavanaatyushna teekshna rooksha vidaahinah; Aahaaraah raajasasyeshtaa duhkhashokaamayapradaah. 9. The foods that are bitter, sour, saline, excessively hot, dry, pungent and burning, are liked by the Rajasic and are productive of pain, grief and disease. Yaatayaamam gatarasam pooti paryushitam cha yat; Ucchishtamapi chaamedhyam bhojanam taamasapriyam. 10. That which is stale, tasteless, putrid, rotten and impure refuse, is the food liked by the Tamasic. Aphalaakaangkshibhiryajno vidhidrishto ya ijyate; Yashtavyameveti manah samaadhaaya sa saattwikah. 11. That sacrifice which is offered by men without desire for reward as enjoined by the ordinance (scripture), with a firm faith that to do so is a duty, is Sattwic (or pure). Abhisandhaaya tu phalam dambhaarthamapi chaiva yat; Ijyate bharatashreshtha tam yajnam viddhi raajasam. 12. The sacrifice which is offered, O Arjuna, seeking a reward and for ostentation, know thou that to be a Rajasic Yajna! Vidhiheenam asrishtaannam mantraheenam adakshinam; Shraddhaavirahitam yajnam taamasam parichakshate. 13. They declare that sacrifice to be Tamasic which is contrary to the ordinances of the scriptures, in which no food is distributed, which is devoid of Mantras and gifts, and which is devoid of faith. 121 BHAGAVAD GITA Devadwijagurupraajna poojanam shauchamaarjavam; Brahmacharyamahimsaa cha shaareeram tapa uchyate. 14. Worship of the gods, the twice-born, the teachers and the wise, purity, straightforwardness, celibacy and non-injury—these are called the austerities of the body. Anudwegakaram vaakyam satyam priyahitam cha yat; Swaadhyaayaabhyasanam chaiva vaangmayam tapa uchyate. 15. Speech which causes no excitement and is truthful, pleasant and beneficial, the practice of the study of the Vedas, are called austerity of speech. COMMENTARY: It is said in the Manu Smriti: "One should speak what is true; one should speak what is pleasant; one should not speak what is true if it is not pleasant, nor what is pleasant if it is false. This is the ancient Dharma". To be an austerity speech should combine all the attributes mentioned in the above verse. Manahprasaadah saumyatwam maunamaatmavinigrahah; Bhaavasamshuddhirityetat tapo maanasamuchyate. 16. Serenity of mind, good-heartedness, purity of nature, self-control—this is called mental austerity. Shraddhayaa parayaa taptam tapastattrividham naraih; Aphalaakaangkshibhiryuktaih saattwikam parichakshate. 17. This threefold austerity practised by steadfast men with the utmost faith, desiring no reward, they call Sattwic. Satkaaramaanapoojaartham tapo dambhena chaiva yat; Kriyate tadiha proktam raajasam chalamadhruvam. 18. The austerity which is practised with the object of gaining good reception, honour and worship and with hypocrisy, is here said to be Rajasic, unstable and transitory. Moodhagraahenaatmano yat peedayaa kriyate tapah; Parasyotsaadanaartham vaa tattaamasamudaahritam. 19. The austerity which is practised out of a foolish notion, with self-torture, or for the purpose of destroying another, is declared to be Tamasic. Daatavyamiti yaddaanam deeyate'nupakaarine; Deshe kaale cha paatre cha taddaanam saattwikam smritam. 20. That gift which is given to one who does nothing in return, knowing it to be a duty to give in a fit place and time to a worthy person, that gift is held to be Sattwic. 122 THE YOGA OF THE DIVISION

OF THE THREEFOLD FAITH Yattu pratyupakaaraartham phalamuddishya vaa punah; Deeyate cha pariklishtam taddaanam raajasam smritam. 21. And, that gift which is made with a view to receive something in return, or looking for a reward, or given reluctantly, is said to be Rajasic. Adeshakaale yaddaanamapaatrebhyashcha deeyate; Asatkritamavajnaatam tattaamasamudaahritam. 22. The gift which is given at the wrong place and time to unworthy persons, without respect or with insult, is declared to be Tamasic. COMMENTARY: At the wrong place and time—at a place which is not holy, where irreligious people and beggars assemble, where wealth acquired through illegal means such as gambling and theft, is distributed to gamblers, singers, fools, rogues, women of evil reputation; wealth that is distributed at an inauspicious time. This does not discourage the giving of alms to the poor. Om tatsaditi nirdesho brahmanas trividhah smritah; Braahmanaastena vedaashcha yajnaashcha vihitaah puraa. 23. "Om Tat Sat": this has been declared to be the triple designation of Brahman. By that were created formerly the Brahmanas, the Vedas and the sacrifices. Tasmaadomityudaahritya yajnadaanatapahkriyaah; Pravartante vidhaanoktaah satatam brahmavaadinaam. 24. Therefore, with the utterance of "Om" are the acts of gift, sacrifice and austerity as enjoined in the scriptures always begun by the students of Brahman. Tadityanabhisandhaaya phalam yajnatapah kriyaah; Daanakriyaashcha vividhaah kriyante mokshakaangkshibhih. 25. Uttering Tat, without aiming at the fruits, are the acts of sacrifice and austerity and the various acts of gift performed by the seekers of liberation. Sadbhaave saadhubhaave cha sadityetatprayujyate; Prashaste karmani tathaa sacchabdah paartha yujyate. 26. The word Sat is used in the sense of reality and of goodness; and so also, O Arjuna, it is used in the sense of an auspicious act! Yajne tapasi daane cha sthitih saditi chochyate; Karma chaiva tadartheeyam sadityevaabhidheeyate. 123 BHAGAVAD GITA 27. Steadfastness in sacrifice, austerity and gift, is also called Sat, and also action in connection with these (or for the sake of the Supreme) is called Sat. Ashraddhayaa hutam dattam tapastaptam kritam cha yat; Asadityuchyate paartha na cha tatpretya no iha. 28. Whatever is sacrificed, given or performed, and whatever austerity is practised without faith, it is called Asat, O Arjuna! It is naught here or hereafter (after death). COMMENTARY: Whatever sacrifice, austerity or charity done without being dedicated to the Lord will be of no avail to the doer in this earthly life here or in the life beyond hereafter. Hari Om Tat Sat Iti Srimad Bhagavadgeetaasoopanishatsu Brahmavidyaayaam

Yogashaastre Sri Krishnaarjunasamvaade Shraddhaatrayavibhaagayogo Naama Saptadasho'dhyaayah Thus in the Upanishads of the glorious Bhagavad Gita, the science of the Eternal, the scripture of Yoga, the dialogue between Sri Krishna and Arjuna, ends the seventeenth discourse entitled: "The Yoga of the Division of the Threefold Faith"

CHAPTER TWENTY-TWO

LIBERATION BY RENUNCIATION Summary of Eighteenth Discourse

The eighteenth discourse, which is the conclusion of the divine discourse of Lord Krishna, is in many ways a summary of the foregoing portions of the Gita. It covers in brief numerous important points dealt with in the previous discourses. Here you behold the ultimate result or effect of the Lord's discourse to Arjuna. The drama of Arjuna's utter despondency and breakdown is finally resolved in triumphant self-mastery, strength and bold resoluteness. Its central message emerges as an assurance that in and through the performance of one's respective duties in life one can qualify for the highest liberation, if one performs actions by renouncing egoism and attachment and surrendering all desire for selfish, personal gain. By regarding the performance of your duties as worship offered to God, you obtain the Grace of the Lord and attain the eternal One. Significantly, this discourse opens with a question by Arjuna asking what is true Sannyasa and true Tyaga (renunciation). In reply to this important and crucial query, the blessed Lord makes it clear to us that real Sannyasa or renunciation lies in renunciation of selfish actions, and even more in the renunciation of the desire or greed for the fruits of any action. Very clearly we are told that selfless and virtuous actions, and actions conducive to the welfare of others should not be abandoned. You must engage yourself in performing such action but renouncing attachment and 124 THE YOGA OF THE DIVISION OF THE THREEFOLD FAITH greed. The true and proper renunciation is giving up of selfishness and attachment while performing one's legitimate duties. This is called Sattwic Tyaga. We neither hate unpleasant action nor are we attached to pleasurable action. As it is not possible for you to renounce all action, the renunciation of egoism, selfishness and attachment in your activity is declared as true renunciation. Karma does not accumulate and bind one who is thus established in such inner renunciation. The divine injunction is that God must be made the sole object of one's life. This is the heart of the Gita gospel. This is the central message in its teaching. This is the one way to your welfare here. Now Sanjaya concludes his narrative by declaring that where there is such obedience as that of Arjuna, and such willing readiness to carry out the divine teachings, there surely prosperity, victory, glory and all blessedness will prevail. Arjuna Uvaacha: Sannyaasasya mahaabaaho tattwamicchaami veditum; Tyaagasya cha hrisheekesha prithak keshinishoodana. Arjuna said: 1. I desire to know severally, O mighty-armed, the essence or truth of renunciation, O Hrishikesa, as also of abandonment, O slayer of Kesi! Sri Bhagavaan Uvaacha: Kaamyaanaam karmanaam nyaasam sannyaasam kavayoviduh; Sarvakarmaphalatyaagam praahustyaagam vichakshanaah. The Blessed Lord said: 2. The sages understand Sannyas to be the renunciation of action with desire; the wise declare the abandonment of the fruits of all actions as Tyaga. Tyaajyam doshavadityeke karma praahurmaneeshinah; Yajnadaanatapah karma na tyaajyamiti chaapare. 3. Some philosophers declare that all actions should be abandoned as an evil, while others declare that acts of gift, sacrifice and austerity should not be relinquished. Nishchayam shrinu me tatra tyaage bharatasattama; Tyaago hi purushavyaaghra trividhah samprakeertitah. 4. Hear from Me the conclusion or the final truth about this abandonment, O best of the Bharatas; abandonment, verily, O best of men, has been declared to be of three kinds! Yajnadaanatapah karma na tyaajyam kaaryameva tat; 125 BHAGAVAD GITA Yajno daanam tapashchaiva paavanaani maneeshinaam. 5. Acts of sacrifice, gift and austerity should not be abandoned, but should be performed; sacrifice, gift and also austerity are the purifiers of the wise. Etaanyapi tu karmaani sangam tyaktwaa phalaani cha; Kartavyaaneeti me paartha nishchitam matamuttamam. 6. But even these actions should be performed leaving aside attachment and the desire for rewards, O Arjuna! This is My certain and best conviction. COMMENTARY: This is a summary of the doctrine of Karma Yoga already enunciated before. The defect in Karma is not in the action itself but in attachment and expectation of a reward. Niyatasya tu sannyaasah karmano nopapadyate; Mohaattasya parityaagas taamasah parikeertitah. 7. Verily, the renunciation of obligatory action is improper; the abandonment of the same from delusion is declared to be Tamasic. Duhkhamityeva yat karma kaayakleshabhayaat tyajet; Sa kritwaa raajasam tyaagam naiva tyaagaphalam labhet. 8. He who abandons action on account of the fear of bodily trouble (because it is painful), he does not obtain the merit of renunciation by doing such Rajasic renunciation. Kaaryamityeva yatkarma niyatam kriyate'rjuna; Sangam tyaktwaa phalam chaiva sa tyaagah saattwiko matah. 9. Whatever obligatory action is done, O Arjuna, merely because it ought to be done, abandoning attachment and also the desire for reward, that renunciation is regarded as Sattwic! Na dweshtyakushalam karma kushale naanushajjate; Tyaagee sattwasamaavishto medhaavee cchinnasamshayah. 10. The man of renunciation, pervaded by purity, intelligent and with his doubts cut asunder, does not hate a disagreeable work nor is he attached to an agreeable one. Na hi dehabhritaa shakyam tyaktum karmaanyasheshatah; Yastu karmaphalatyaagi sa tyaageetyabhidheeyate. 11. Verily, it is not possible for an embodied being to abandon actions entirely; but he who relinquishes the rewards of actions is verily called a man of renunciation. COMMENTARY: Nature, and your own nature, too, will urge you to do actions. You will have to abandon the idea of agency and the fruits of actions. Then no action will bind you. 126 THE YOGA OF LIBERATION BY RENUNCIATION Anishtamishtam mishram cha trividham karmanah phalam; Bhavatyatyaaginaam pretya na tu sannyaasinaam kwachit. 12. The threefold fruit of action—evil, good and mixed—accrues after death to the non-abandoners, but never to the abandoners. Panchaitaani mahaabaaho kaaranaani nibodha me; Saankhye kritaante proktaani siddhaye sarvakarmanaam. 13. Learn from Me, O mighty-armed Arjuna, these five causes, as declared in the Sankhya system for the accomplishment of all actions! Adhishthaanam tathaa kartaa karanam cha prithagvidham; Vividhaashcha prithakcheshtaa daivam chaivaatra panchamam. 14. The body, the doer, the various senses, the different functions of various sorts, and the presiding Deity, also, the fifth, Shareeravaangmanobhiryat karma praarabhate narah; Nyaayyam vaa vipareetam vaa panchaite tasya hetavah. 15. Whatever action a man performs by his body, speech and mind, whether right or the reverse, these five are its causes. Tatraivam sati kartaaram aatmaanam kevalam tu yah; Pashyatyakritabuddhitwaan na sa pashyati durmatih. 16. Now, such being the case, he who, owing to untrained understanding, looks upon his Self, which is isolated, as the agent, he of perverted intelligence, sees not. Yasya naahankrito bhaavo buddhiryasya na lipyate; Hatwaapi sa imaam llokaan na hanti na nibadhyate. 17. He who is ever free from the egoistic notion, whose intelligence is not tainted by (good or evil), though he slays these people, he slayeth not, nor is he bound (by the action). Jnaanam jneyam parijnaataa trividhaa karmachodanaa; Karanam karma karteti trividhah karmasangrahah. 18. Knowledge, the knowable and the knower form the threefold impulse to action; the organ, the action and the agent form the threefold basis of action. Jnaanam karma cha kartaa cha tridhaiva gunabhedatah; Prochyate gunasankhyaane yathaavacchrinu taanyapi. 127 BHAGAVAD GITA 19. Knowledge, action and the actor are declared in the science of the Gunas (the Sankhya philosophy) to be of three kinds only, according to the distinction of the Gunas. Hear them also duly. Sarvabhooteshu yenaikam bhaavamavyayameekshate; Avibhaktam vibhakteshu tajjnaanam viddhi saattwikam. 20. That by which one sees the one indestructible Reality in all beings, not separate in all the separate beings—know thou that knowledge to be Sattwic (pure). Prithaktwena tu yajjnaanam naanaabhaavaan prithagvidhaan; Vetti sarveshu bhooteshu tajjnaanam viddhi raajasam. 21. But that knowledge which sees in all beings various entities of distinct kinds as different from one another—know thou that knowledge to be Rajasic (passionate). Yattu kritsnavadekasmin kaarye saktamahaitukam; Atattwaarthavadalpam cha tattaamasamudaahritam. 22. But that which clings to one single effect as if it were the whole, without reason, without foundation in Truth, and trivial—that is declared to be Tamasic (dark). Niyatam sangarahitam araagadweshatah kritam; Aphalaprepsunaa karma yattat saattwikamuchyate. 23. An action which is ordained, which is free from attachment, which is done without love or hatred by one who is not desirous of any reward—that action is declared to be Sattwic. Yattu kaamepsunaa karma saahankaarena vaa punah; Kriyate bahulaayaasam tadraajasamudaahritam. 24. But that action which is done by one longing for the fulfilment of desires or gain, with egoism or with much effort—that is declared to be Rajasic. Anubandham kshayam himsaam anavekshya cha paurusham; Mohaadaarabhyate karma yattat taamasamuchyate. 25. That action which is undertaken from delusion, without regard to the consequences of loss, injury and (one's own) ability—that is declared to be Tamasic. Muktasango'nahamvaadi dhrityutsaahasamanvitah; Siddhyasiddhyor nirvikaarah kartaa saattwika uchyate. 26. He who is free from attachment, non-egoistic, endowed with firmness and enthusiasm and unaffected by success or failure, is called Sattwic. 128 THE YOGA OF

LIBERATION BY RENUNCIATION Raagee karmaphalaprepsur lubdho himsaatmako'shuchih; Harshashokaanvitah kartaa raajasah parikeertitah. 27. Passionate, desiring to obtain the rewards of actions, cruel, greedy, impure, moved by joy and sorrow, such an agent is said to be Rajasic. Ayuktah praakritah stabdhah shatho naishkritiko'lasah; Vishaadee deerghasootree cha kartaa taamasa uchyate. 28. Unsteady, dejected, unbending, cheating, malicious, vulgar, lazy and proscrastinating—such an agent is called Tamasic. Buddherbhedam dhriteshchaiva gunatastrividham shrinu; Prochyamaanamasheshena prithaktwena dhananjaya. 29. Hear thou the threefold division of the intellect and firmness according to the Gunas, as I declare them fully and distinctly, O Arjuna! Pravrittim cha nivrittim cha karyaakaarye bhayaabhaye; Bandhammoksham cha yaa vetti buddhih saa paartha saattwikee. 30. That which knows the path of work and renunciation, what ought to be done and what ought not to be done, fear and fearlessness, bondage and liberation—that intellect is Sattwic, O Arjuna! Yayaa dharmamadharmam cha kaaryam chaakaaryameva cha; Ayathaavat prajaanaati buddhih saa paartha raajasee. 31. That by which one incorrectly understands Dharma and Adharma, and also what ought to be done and what ought not to be done—that intellect, O Arjuna, is Rajasic! COMMENTARY: That which is ordained in the scriptures is Dharma. That which hurls you into the abyss of ignorance is Adharma. The Rajasic intellect is not able to distinguish between righteous and unrighteous actions. Adharmam dharmamiti yaa manyate tamasaavritaa; Sarvaarthaan vipareetaamshcha buddhih saa paartha taamasee. 32. That which, enveloped in darkness, views Adharma as Dharma and all things perverted—that intellect, O Arjuna, is called Tamasic! Dhrityaa yayaa dhaarayate manah praanendriyakriyaah; Yogenaavyabhichaarinyaa dhritih saa paartha saattwikee. 33. The unwavering firmness by which, through Yoga, the functions of the mind, the life-force and the senses are restrained—that firmness, O Arjuna, is Sattwic! 129 BHAGAVAD GITA Yayaa tu dharmakaamaarthaan dhrityaa dhaarayate'rjuna; Prasangena phalaakaangkshee dhritih saa paartha raajasee. 34. But that firmness, O Arjuna, by which, on account of attachment and desire for reward, one holds fast to Dharma, enjoyment of pleasures and earning of wealth—that firmness, O Arjuna, is Rajasic! Yayaa swapnam bhayam shokam vishaadam madameva cha; Na vimunchati durmedhaa dhritih saa paartha taamasee. 35. That by which a stupid man does not abandon sleep, fear, grief, despair and also conceit—that firmness, O Arjuna, is Tamasic! Sukham twidaaneem trividham shrinu me bharatarshabha; Abhyaasaadramate yatra duhkhaantam cha nigacchati. 36. Now hear from Me, O Arjuna, of the threefold pleasure, in which one rejoices by practice and surely comes to the end of pain! Yattadagre vishamiva parinaame'mritopamam; Tatsukham saattwikam proktam aatmabuddhiprasaadajam. 37. That which is like poison at first but in the end like nectar—that pleasure is declared to be Sattwic, born of the purity of one's own mind due to Self-realisation. Vishayendriya samyogaad yattadagre'mritopamam; Parinaame vishamiva tatsukham raajasam smritam. 38. That pleasure which arises from the contact of the sense-organs with the objects, which is at first like nectar and in the end like poison—that is declared to be Rajasic. Yadagre chaanubandhe cha sukham mohanamaatmanah; Nidraalasyapramaadottham tattaamasamudaahritam. 39. That pleasure which at first and in the sequel is delusive of the self, arising from sleep, indolence and heedlessness—such a pleasure is declared to be Tamasic. Na tadasti prithivyaam vaa divi deveshu vaa punah; Sattwam prakritijairmuktam yadebhih syaat tribhirgunaih. 40. There is no being on earth or again in heaven among the gods that is liberated from the three qualities born of Nature. Braahmanakshatriyavishaam shoodraanaam cha parantapa; Karmaani pravibhaktaani swabhaavaprabhavairgunaih. 130 THE YOGA OF LIBERATION BY RENUNCIATION 41. Of Brahmanas, Kshatriyas and Vaishyas, as also the Sudras, O Arjuna, the duties are distributed according to the qualities born of their own nature! Shamo damastapah shaucham kshaantiraarjavameva cha; Jnaanam vijnaanam aastikyam brahmakarma swabhaavajam. 42. Serenity, self-restraint, austerity, purity, forgiveness and also uprightness, knowledge, realisation and belief in God are the duties of the Brahmanas, born of (their own) nature. Shauryam tejo dhritirdaakshyam yuddhe chaapyapalaayanam; Daanameeshwarabhaavashcha kshaatram karmaswabhaavajam. 43. Prowess, splendour, firmness, dexterity and also not fleeing from battle, generosity and lordliness are the duties of Kshatriyas, born of (their own) nature. Krishigaurakshyavaanijyam vaishyakarma swabhaavajam; Paricharyaatmakam karma shoodrasyaapi swabhaavajam. 44. Agriculture, cattle-rearing and trade are the duties of the Vaishya (merchant class), born of (their own) nature; and action consisting of service is the duty of the Sudra (servant class), born of (their own) nature. COMMENTARY: When a man does his duties rightly according to his order of life, his heart gets purified and he goes to heaven. Swe swe karmanyabhiratah samsiddhim labhate narah; Swakarmaniratah siddhim yathaa vindati tacchrinu. 45. Each man, devoted to his own duty, attains perfection. How he attains perfection while being engaged in his own duty, hear now. Yatah pravrittirbhootaanaam yena sarvamidam tatam; Swakarmanaa tamabhyarchya siddhim vindati maanavah. 46. He from whom all the beings have evolved and by whom all this is pervaded, worshipping Him with his own duty, man attains perfection. COMMENTARY: Man attains perfection by worshipping the Lord through the performance of his own duty, that is, he becomes qualified for the dawn of Self-knowledge. Shreyaanswadharmo vigunah paradharmaat swanushthitaat; Swabhaavaniyatam karma kurvannaapnoti kilbisham. 47. Better is one's own duty (though) destitute of merits, than the duty of another well performed. He who does the duty ordained by his own nature incurs no sin. 131 BHAGAVAD GITA Sahajam karma kaunteya sadoshamapi na tyajet; Sarvaarambhaa hi doshena dhoomenaagnirivaavritaah. 48. One should not abandon, O Arjuna, the duty to which one is born, though faulty; for, all undertakings are enveloped by evil, as fire by smoke! Asaktabuddhih sarvatra jitaatmaa vigatasprihah; Naishkarmyasiddhim paramaam sannyaasenaadhigacchati. 49. He whose intellect is unattached everywhere, who has subdued his self, from whom desire has fled,—he by renunciation attains the supreme state of freedom from action. Siddhim praapto yathaa brahma tathaapnoti nibodha me; Samaasenaiva kaunteya nishthaa jnaanasya yaa paraa. 50. Learn from Me in brief, O Arjuna, how he who has attained perfection reaches Brahman, that supreme state of knowledge. Buddhyaa vishuddhayaa yukto dhrityaatmaanam niyamya cha; Shabdaadeen vishayaanstyaktwaa raagadweshau vyudasya cha. 51. Endowed with a pure intellect, controlling the self by firmness, relinquishing sound and other objects and abandoning both hatred and attraction, Viviktasevee laghwaashee yatavaakkaayamaanasah; Dhyaanayogaparo nityam vairaagyam samupaashritah. 52. Dwelling in solitude, eating but little, with speech, body and mind subdued, always engaged in concentration and meditation, taking refuge in dispassion, Ahankaaram balam darpam kaamam krodham parigraham; Vimuchya nirmamah shaanto brahmabhooyaaya kalpate. 53. Having abandoned egoism, strength, arrogance, anger, desire, and covetousness, free from the notion of "mine" and peaceful,—he is fit for becoming Brahman. Brahmabhootah prasannaatmaa na shochati na kaangkshati; Samah sarveshu bhooteshu madbhaktim labhate paraam. 54. Becoming Brahman, serene in the Self, he neither grieves nor desires; the same to all beings, he attains supreme devotion unto Me. Bhaktyaa maamabhijaanaati yaavaanyashchaasmi tattwatah; Tato maam tattwato jnaatwaa vishate tadanantaram. 132 THE YOGA OF LIBERATION BY RENUNCIATION 55. By devotion he knows Me in truth, what and who I am; and knowing Me in truth, he forthwith enters into the Supreme. Sarvakarmaanyapi sadaa kurvaano madvyapaashrayah; Matprasaadaadavaapnoti shaashwatam padamavyayam. 56. Doing all actions always, taking refuge in Me, by My Grace he obtains the eternal, indestructible state or abode. Chetasaa sarvakarmaani mayi sannyasya matparah; Buddhiyogam upaashritya macchittah satatam bhava. 57. Mentally renouncing all actions in Me, having Me as the highest goal, resorting to the Yoga of discrimination do thou ever fix thy mind on Me. Macchittah sarvadurgaani matprasaadaat tarishyasi; Atha chet twam ahankaaraan na shroshyasi vinangkshyasi. 58. Fixing thy mind on Me, thou shalt by My Grace overcome all obstacles; but if from egoism thou wilt not hear Me, thou shalt perish. Yadahankaaram aashritya na yotsya iti manyase; Mithyaisha vyavasaayaste prakritistwaam niyokshyati. 59. If, filled with egoism, thou thinkest: "I will not fight", vain is this, thy resolve; Nature will compel thee. Swabhaavajena kaunteya nibaddhah swena karmanaa; Kartum necchasi yanmohaat karishyasyavasho'pi tat. 60. O Arjuna, bound by thy own Karma (action) born of thy own nature, that which from delusion thou wishest not to do, even that thou shalt do helplessly! COMMENTARY: Thou wilt be forced to fight because of thy nature. It will compel thee to fight, much against thy will. Eeshwarah sarvabhootaanaam hriddeshe'rjuna tishthati; Bhraamayan sarvabhootaani yantraaroodhaani maayayaa. 61. The Lord dwells in the hearts of all beings, O Arjuna, causing all beings, by His illusive power, to revolve as if mounted on a machine! Tameva sharanam gaccha sarvabhaavena bhaarata; Tatprasaadaatparaam shaantim sthaanam praapsyasi shaashwatam. 133 BHAGAVAD GITA 62. Fly unto Him for refuge with all thy being, O Arjuna! By His Grace thou shalt obtain supreme peace and the eternal abode. Iti te jnaanamaakhyaatam guhyaad guhyataram mayaa; Vimrishyaitadasheshena yathecchasi tathaa kuru. 63. Thus has wisdom more secret than secrecy itself been declared unto thee by Me; having reflected over it fully, then act thou as thou wishest. Sarvaguhyatamam bhooyah shrinu me paramam vachah; Ishto'si me dridhamiti tato vakshyaami te hitam. 64. Hear thou again My supreme word, most secret of all; because thou art dearly beloved of Me, I will tell thee what is good. Manmanaa bhava madbhakto madyaajee maam namaskuru;

Maamevaishyasi satyam te pratijaane priyo'si me. 65. Fix thy mind on Me, be devoted to Me, sacrifice to Me, bow down to Me. Thou shalt come even to Me; truly do I promise unto thee, (for) thou art dear to Me. Sarvadharmaan parityajya maamekam sharanam vraja; Aham twaa sarvapaapebhyo mokshayishyaami maa shuchah. 66. Abandoning all duties, take refuge in Me alone; I will liberate thee from all sins; grieve not. Idam te naatapaskaaya naabhaktaaya kadaachana; Na chaashushrooshave vaachyam na cha maam yo'bhyasooyati. 67. This is never to be spoken by thee to one who is devoid of austerities, to one who is not devoted, nor to one who does not render service, nor who does not desire to listen, nor to one who cavils at Me. Ya imam paramam guhyam madbhakteshvabhidhaasyati; Bhaktim mayi paraam kritwaa maamevaishyatyasamshayah. 68. He who with supreme devotion to Me will teach this supreme secret to My devotees, shall doubtless come to Me. Na cha tasmaanmanushyeshu kashchinme priyakrittamah; Bhavitaa na cha me tasmaadanyah priyataro bhuvi. 69. Nor is there any among men who does dearer service to Me, nor shall there be another on earth dearer to Me than he. 134 THE YOGA OF LIBERATION BY RENUNCIATION COMMENTARY: He who hands down this Gita to My devotees does immense service to Me. He is extremely dear to Me. In the present generation, there will be none dearer to Me in the world, nor shall there be in the future also. Adhyeshyate cha ya imam dharmyam samvaadamaavayoh; Jnaanayajnena tenaaham ishtah syaamiti me matih. 70. And he who will study this sacred dialogue of ours, by him I shall have been worshipped by the sacrifice of wisdom; such is My conviction. Shraddhaavaan anasooyashcha shrinuyaadapi yo narah; So'pi muktah shubhaamllokaan praapnuyaat punyakarmanaam. 71. The man also who hears this, full of faith and free from malice, he, too, liberated, shall attain to the happy worlds of those of righteous deeds. Kacchid etacchrutam paartha twayaikaagrena chetasaa; Kacchid ajnaanasammohah pranashtaste dhananjaya. 72. Has this been heard, O Arjuna, with one-pointed mind? Has the delusion of thy ignorance been fully destroyed, O Dhananjaya? Arjuna Uvaacha: Nashto mohah smritirlabdhaa twatprasaadaanmayaachyuta; Sthito'smi gata sandehah karishye vachanam tava. Arjuna said: 73. Destroyed is my delusion as I have gained my memory (knowledge) through Thy Grace, O Krishna! I am firm; my doubts are gone. I will act according to Thy word. Sanjaya Uvaacha: Ityaham vaasudevasya paarthasya cha mahaatmanah; Samvaadam imam ashrausham adbhutam romaharshanam. Sanjaya said: 74. Thus have I heard this wonderful dialogue between

Krishna and the high-souled Arjuna, which causes the hair to stand on end. Vyaasaprasaadaacchrutavaan etadguhyamaham param; Yogam yogeshwaraat krishnaat saakshaat kathayatah swayam. 75. Through the Grace of Vyasa I have heard this supreme and most secret Yoga direct from Krishna, the Lord of Yoga Himself declaring it. 135 BHAGAVAD GITA Raajan samsmritya samsmritya samvaadam imam adbhutam; Keshavaarjunayoh punyam hrishyaami cha muhurmuhuh. 76. O King, remembering this wonderful and holy dialogue between Krishna and Arjuna, I rejoice again and again! Taccha samsmritya samsmritya roopamatyadbhutam hareh; Vismayo me mahaan raajan hrishyaami cha punah punah. 77. And remembering again and again also that most wonderful form of Hari, great is my wonder, O King! And I rejoice again and again! Yatra yogeshwarah krishno yatra paartho dhanurdharah; Tatra shreervijayo bhootirdhruvaa neetirmatirmama. 78. Wherever there is Krishna, the Lord of Yoga, wherever there is Arjuna, the archer, there are prosperity, happiness, victory and firm policy; such is my conviction. Hari Om Tat Sat Iti Srimad Bhagavadgeetaasoopanishatsu Brahmavidyaayaam Yogashaastre Sri Krishnaarjunasamvaade Mokshasannyaasayogo Naama Ashtaadasho'dhyaayah Thus in the Upanishads of the glorious Bhagavad Gita, the science of the Eternal, the scripture of Yoga, the dialogue between Sri Krishna and Arjuna, ends the eighteenth discourse entitled: "The Liberation by Renunciation" Om Shanti! Shanti! Shanti!